THE 12 GREATEST ROUNDS OF BOXING

THE 12 GREATEST ROUNDS OF BOXING

THE UNTOLD STORIES

FERDIE PACHECO, M.D.
WITH
JIM MOSKOVITZ

Robson Books

First published in Great Britain in 2001 by Robson Books,
10 Blenheim Court, Brewery Road, London N7 9NY

A member of the Chrysalis Group plc

First published in the USA by Total Sports Illustrated, New York

Book design: Chad Lawrence

British Library Cataloguing in Publications Data
A catalogue record for this title is available from the British Library

ISBN 1 86105 450 5

Printed in Great Britain by Bell & Bain Ltd., Glasgow

CONTENTS

ACKNOWLEDGMENTS

This book could not have been produced without the massive efforts of my wife, Luisita, who provided assistance with research and typing, the use of several of her photographs, and incredible emotional support.

My life in boxing I owe to Chris Dundee and Angelo Dundee, who permitted me into the sport's inner sanctum for 40 years and allowed me the undistilled pleasure of working in the corners of great champions, Muhammad Ali in particular, as well as four-round pugs.

My life as a sportscaster I owe to my agent, Barry Frank, who placed me at NBC, and to Don Ohlmeyer, who left me there for more than 10 years. My 14 years at Showtime Networks I owe to Jay Larkin, who forged a great broadcast team.

Finally, I owe a great thank-you to Jim Moskovitz, who pushed this book and a TV special into fruition by dint of his persuasiveness and hard work. Thanks also go to the book's editor, George Pattison.

FERDIE PACHECO, M.D.

My contributions to this book are dedicated to the loving memory of Dr. Mayer Moskovitz, and this book would not have been possible without the persistent and creative efforts of my wife, Joyce Moskovitz.

I also wish to acknowledge Jay Larkin, Ann Gilmor, Jerry Offsay, Mark Zacharin, David Stern, Joan Cox, and Showtime for their support of the television special "The 12 Greatest Rounds of Boxing," which provided much of the research and the original interviews for this book. Special thanks go to Emanuel Steward, Mills Lane, Roger Kahn, Tom Hauser, Teddy Atlas, Lou Duva, and Angelo Dundee for their insightful interviews and to boxing historian Hank Kaplan for providing valuable research assistance and access to photographs.

Kudos also go to Shari Chertok and Re:Search for their wonderful archival work and to Sam Chapin, whose excellent and affordable word processing made this book possible.

JAMES L. MOSKOVITZ

FOREWORD

It is a pleasure to introduce my good friend Ferdie Pacheco's account of the 12 rounds of boxing that he rates as the greatest ever.

Few people know boxing as Ferdie does. For decades he has been a fixture on the scene, first as a physician and cornerman for Muhammad Ali and other world champions, then as the television analyst known around the world as the Fight Doctor. Boxing fans know, of course, that their sport involves much more than controlled violence. Fights are also a battle of wits and tactics, and this can make for a beautiful spectacle. That brings me back to Ferdie Pacheco, who as an accomplished artist can appreciate the beauty of boxing. I have in my office a painting he made for me of a scene from the book (and television movie) *Lonesome Dove*. In fact, Ferdie always calls me Lonesome Dove because he says I look like one of the story's characters.

You might expect that some of history's great heavyweights would appear in a book about boxing's greatest rounds, and indeed, heavyweight legends play a big role in the pages that follow. One of the encounters chronicled by Ferdie is the first round of Jack Dempsey's epic fight with Jess Willard. Some people have argued that Jack's hands were "loaded" with plaster of paris. Yeah, right. What was in those gloves was Jack Dempsey's fists, and big Jess found out just how hard the Manassa Mauler hit.

You'll also read about the first round of the second Joe Louis–Max Schmeling fight, which took place in 1938. Louis's quiet dignity had done much to soothe the anger and tensions that had arisen when white America was confronted with its first black heavyweight champion, Jack Johnson, in the early years of the century. The Louis-Schmeling fight came at a crucial time in history—when Adolf Hitler sought to make Schmeling an example of the "master race" that Hitler believed he could create. Schmeling, who was not of Hitler's ilk, was an unfortunate pawn in the fuhrer's scheme. Louis of course beat Schmeling, and later in life these two adversaries became friends.

Louis also had to get it on with a young Irishman named Billy Conn, whom he outweighed by almost 25 pounds but who damned near beat him. Billy was winning when he provoked an exchange with Joe in the 13th round in hopes of securing a knockout—but instead the lights went out for Billy. Later, Conn reportedly asked Louis why he didn't "lend him the title" while Louis was in the army. Joe supposedly replied, "Billy, I lent it to you for 13 rounds, but you couldn't hang on to it."

Four of Muhammad Ali's fights, including two with Sonny Liston, are described here. In the first, Ali, then known as Cassius Clay, claimed that an illegal substance on Liston's gloves or body had been rubbed into his eye. Angelo Dundee, his trainer, pushed Ali off the stool, instructing him to keep moving. Ali danced until his eyes cleared. Liston, who allegedly had underworld contacts, quit in his corner at the end of the seventh round. Most people in boxing weren't alarmed by Liston's supposed underworld connections, but they couldn't forgive his not going out like a champion. In an article by the late, great sportswriter Jimmy Cannon, Billy Conn was reported to have called Liston a "dog."

Jersey Joe Walcott was assigned to referee the second Ali-Liston fight. Walcott had been a good fighter in his day, but he was definitely in over his head as a referee. As detailed in Ferdie's account, in the opening round Ali put Liston down with a short right hand, then stood over his opponent, taunting him, instead of going to a neutral corner as required. Jersey Joe didn't seem to know what to do. Confusion reigned. Amid the chaos Ali eventually was declared the winner. This fight is a great example of why a competent referee is an absolute necessity—for any fight, but especially for a championship bout.

One of boxing's great cornermen, Eddie Futch, exemplified how the cornerman's job should be done by the way he handled Joe Frazier in the "Thrilla in Manila" with Ali. Eddie refused to let Joe, who was badly battered, come out for the 15th round. Joe was in no condition to go on; the consequences might have been grave if he had continued. The three fights between Ali and Frazier were titanic battles, and their rivalry ranks as one of history's greatest.

The 12 Greatest Rounds of Boxing would not be complete without an entry showcasing the man who was probably the greatest pound-for-pound fighter of all time, Sugar Ray Robinson. Robinson could box your ears off or knock you out with one shot, in addition to being a superior ring general. All of his greatness was on display in Round 13 in his 1951 TKO of Jake LaMotta for the middleweight championship.

Another of the book's highlights is Ferdie's description of the 1985 middleweight bout between Marvelous Marvin Hagler and Thomas Hearns—a fight that many people, myself included, consider the greatest they ever saw. In Round 1 they went toe to toe from bell to bell. Hagler constantly pressed forward, "hands up, chin down," and took all that Hearns could throw. This was fighting at its best. My slogan, "Let's Get It On," describes just what they did: They got it on!

This book reports what professional prizefighting is really all about. Every boxing fan will thoroughly enjoy it.

MILLS LANE

THE 12 GREATEST
ROUNDS OF BOXING

BEGINNINGS AND BACKGROUND

In my life I have had three main interests: my profession, the practice of medicine; my hobby, the Civil War; and my avocation, the sweet science of boxing.

This book is the result of a lifelong love affair with the daffy but often exhilarating world of boxing.

It began on a hot afternoon in August 1937 when I was passing the time playing baseball in the redbrick streets of Tampa, Florida. I was nine years old and, like all of the kids on my block, a sports fanatic, which in that primitive day meant we *played* the games rather than watched them. Youngsters of today might find that a strange concept.

My game that day was interrupted by my father, J.B. who arrived home from work with some sense of urgency and commanded me to change immediately into my Sunday best.

This was an enormous shock to me, since my father had never before been seen in our neighborhood between breakfast and supper. He owned a drugstore and was simply never around to take me anywhere, much less in the middle of the day.

To my considerable shock, he took me to the Columbia Restaurant, Tampa's finest dining establishment, where my aunt Lola was the head cashier.

The Fonda, the restaurant's main daytime dining salon, was

closed, as lunch hour had long since passed. Seated at a table in that room, talking to the owner, Lawrence Hernandez, was a huge man. We marched up and my dad, gently prodded me toward him.

"Champ, this is my son Ferdie," he said. "Ferdie, this is the heavyweight champion of the world." Dad didn't have to tell me that. I had photos of this man on my bedroom wall.

Imagine! Jack Dempsey, right there in Tampa, in the Columbia Restaurant! He took my small hand and shook it with a smile. His hands were huge and hard.

"He knows all about boxing. He reads *The Ring* magazine cover to cover every month," said my father to the champ. I was amazed to hear that Dad knew such things about me. He never seemed to be around.

"Oh yeah, tell me something you know about boxing," Dempsey said, acting like he doubted my dad.

"I know all about The Long Count . . . ," I began, and Dempsey laughed out loud.

"I believe you. You do know about boxing. Have you et yet?" he asked. Dempsey's voice was high pitched, kind of like a girl's.

"No, sir."

"Well, belly up, young feller. We'll split an arroz con pollo."

Chicken and yellow rice was the gustatory equivalent of gold at the Columbia—a rare treat.

In a flash a waiter who was called El Rey, because he looked like King Alfonso of Spain, brought in the delicacy and two forks. The Champ and I dug in and ate ravenously until we had finished the entire dish. It took Gene Tunney longer to get off the deck than it did for us to polish off that plate.

Dempsey brushed the bread crumbs off his vest and my suit and stood me up in front of him.

"I got something for you, so you won't forget me," he said.

As if I would forget this, the most impressive thing that had happened to me in all my nine years!

Then Dempsey produced a small pair of boxing gloves. They were made of gold and had a string with a golden tassel with which to attach them to a key chain. On the front of the gloves were embossed the letters JD.

"You won't lose them, will you, champ?" he said, patting me on the shoulder. Then he shocked me with a playful left hook to my jaw. "Protect yourself at all times," the heavyweight champion of the world advised me.

From that moment on, my JD gloves never left my key chain—through high school, college, medical school, a war, and decades of prizefights. One night, however, while beating a hasty retreat in the midst of some domestic infelicity, I left them in my cuff-link box. The ensuing divorce was acrimonious. I won the house and custody of my kids, but I lost the golden JD gloves. What a tragedy!

So I date my long, fierce interest in boxing to that day in 1937 when I shared a dish of arroz con pollo with Jack Dempsey at the Columbia. This book is directly the result of that memorable lunch.

In 1959 I was leading the hard life of a medical intern at Mt. Sinai Hospital in Miami Beach. For a diversion, I wangled the job of providing medical coverage for the fights held at the Miami Beach Auditorium, striking up a loose arrangement with promoter Chris Dundee, an aggressive entrepreneur. In turn I got to know Angelo, his baby brother, who would become known as one of boxing's great manager-trainer-cut men. Angelo had already made a name for himself through his management of an eye injury suffered by Carmen Basilio in a middleweight title fight with Sugar Ray Robinson. The Dundees' boxing activities were based at Miami Beach's 5th Street Gym.

When I became a licensed physician in 1960, I opened a charity clinic in the Overtown district of Miami. The area was known as the Swamp, and its population was mainly black. Segregation was still widespread at the time in Miami, and white doctors avoided mixing white and black patients in their waiting rooms. Chris Dundee saw in my clinic an opportunity to obtain medical care for his black fighters, and I was happy to oblige.

My boxing practice grew as numerous excellent boxers fled their native Cuba and fell into the welcoming arms of Angelo Dundee. To accommodate this influx of exiles, I opened a "Cuban" branch of my practice on Southwest 8th Street, which is known in the Little Havana section of Miami as the Trail. Chris's fighters, whether white, black, or Hispanic, could now be assured of getting good medical treatment in a friendly setting at one or another of my offices. Even better, as far as Chris was concerned, I didn't charge his boxers a dime for my services. It was a fair swap between Chris and me: He gave me an entrée into the inside world of boxing; I provided free medical care to the denizens of his 5th Street Gym. This mutually blissful arrangement lasted until I hopped off the "Ali Circus," retiring as a cornerman-physician to Ali in 1977. (Chris Dundee died in 1998, at age 92. To this day I stay in close touch with Angelo Dundee and his wife, Helen, and their two children. In fact, Angelo is the godfather of my daughter, Tina.)

My years as a cornerman were spent taking care of Angelo Dundee's boxers, 12 of whom—including Muhammad Ali—became world champions. Actually, since I did not charge a fee for my medical services, I became the doctor for any fighter passing through the 5th Street Gym. I filled that role for two wonderful decades, during which I met many of the great old characters of boxing and listened to hundreds of their tales.

In my time I had the good fortune to absorb the wit and wisdom of trainers like Lou Gross, "Sellout" Moe Fleischer (his fights set records for sellout crowds in the 1920s in New York), Allie Ridgeway, Chickie Ferrara, Freddie Brown, Ray Arcel, and so many others who spent their lives in the ring corners and gyms of the world.

The characters I met at the 5th Street Gym exhibited enough bizarre behavior to fill several sitcoms. Take, for example, tiny Sully the Gatekeeper, who tried to collect a quarter from anyone who came up the stairs to the gym. Once he had the nerve to try to extract his two bits from hulking, smoldering Sonny Liston.

"Twenty-five cents, you mud turtle," chirped Sully.

Sonny eyed him with his meanest killer look.

"Somebody get this *half* motherfucker out of my face," growled Liston.

Then there was Evil Eye Finkle, who for a "finsky" (five dollars) would put the whammy on your opponent. For a "double finster" or "tenner" he would apply his guaranteed double whammy. He got so good (and famous) at this that he appeared as a regular character, Evil Eye Fleagle, in Al Capp's *L'il Abner* comic strip.

The coming of winter brought the big fights to Miami Beach, which in turn brought crowds of tourists from the north. Kingfish Levinsky, a well-worn heavyweight whose claim to fame was that he was once flattened by Joe Louis in one of the champ's "bum of the month" bouts, was part of the local winter scene. Kingfish had a mashed-up face and an intimidating presence that made buying a $5 tie for $25 seem like a reasonable proposition. If anyone objected, Kingfish said menacingly, "My sister made that tie with her own hands." Celebrities such as Frank Sinatra and Jackie Gleason usually bought three ties, telling Kingfish to keep the change from a C-note.

There was also a man called Raincoat Levine, whose connections with boxing were obscure. He never appeared in the 5th Street Gym without wearing a raincoat. When someone challenged his chosen attire, saying, "The sun is shining; it don't look like it's going to rain," Levine would reply, "It might."

The Dundees' gym would fill up with the great boxing writers from up North. Giants like Budd Schulberg, Ring Lardner, Jim Bishop, Jesse Abramson, Barney Nagler, Red Smith, Jerry Lisker, and Dave Anderson would mix with local standouts such as Ed Pope, Gary Long, Howard Kleinberg, John Crittenden, and Tom Archdeacon and the irrepressible boxing announcer and radio personality "Colonel" Bob Sheridan. It was a time of long lunches filled with long and plentiful boxing short stories, enough to fill the Damon Runyon library.

Upon leaving the inside-the-ropes part of the boxing world in 1977, I slid easily behind a microphone and began work as NBC-TV's boxing consultant and on-camera analyst. I subsequently shifted over to Showtime cable television's boxing productions, which I covered for 14 years.

So this book embodies a lifetime's involvement in boxing at every level, from my days as a wide-eyed nine-year-old meeting Jack Dempsey, through 20 years as a cornerman to world champions and a physician treating fighters, to my work analyzing the sport for the television audience. It has been a wonderful ride in an Alice in Wonderland world. I hope that in presenting my choice of boxing's 12 greatest rounds, this book also conveys the flavor and color of that wild, wonderful ride.

My choice of the 12 greatest rounds of boxing is based on the following criteria:

1. Rounds that had a significant, lasting effect on the rules of boxing. Examples are the 1919 Jess Willard–Jack Dempsey fight and the Dempsey–Gene Tunney "long count" of 1927.
2. Rounds that affected a fighter's career, for example, the "Blindness Round" (Round 5) of the 1964 Cassius Clay–Sonny Liston fight
3. Rounds of international importance beyond their boxing significance, for instance, Joe Louis vs. Max Schmeling in 1938
4. Rounds in which life and death hung in the balance and in the atmosphere, as was the case when Sugar Ray Robinson clashed with Jake LaMotta in 1951 and Muhammad Ali met Joe Frazier in Manila in 1975.

It so happens that at least one of my 12 greatest rounds covers each decade of the last century from the teens through the 1980s. Also, and not surprisingly, great fights and great rounds usually involve great fighters, and such is the case here. Many of history's top boxers were the protagonists in these memorable rounds.

The book's "untold stories" come from my lifetime of listening to boxing insiders. These men of reputation include many from the modern era, such as Angelo Dundee, Emanuel Steward, Mills Lane, Lou Duva, Eddie Futch, Thomas Hauser, Roger Kahn, and Teddy Atlas. The witnesses to the great fights of earlier days are old-timers like Abe Attell and Doc Kearns, who would spend their later years telling tales of "trickeration"—how they fixed fights or played various other dirty (but usually fascinating and unforgettable) tricks. Some of these yarns are reported here with the same grain of salt with which I first took them, but most have at least a semblance of credibility.

So, consider this book an entertainment based on what I have heard, what I have seen, what I have done, and what I have reported from ringside during my years in boxing. Some people might choose differently when it comes to boxing's 12 greatest rounds, and good arguments can be made in favor of other rounds, but these are *my* 12 greatest rounds.

Heavyweight champion Jack Dempsey, dubbed "the Modern Apollo," in a 1922 portrait
(*AP/Wide World Photos*)

THE MASSACRE

JACK DEMPSEY vs. JESS WILLARD

CHALLENGER   **CHAMPION**

HEAVYWEIGHT CHAMPIONSHIP

JULY 4, 1919
TOLEDO, OHIO

ROUND I

Behind every great fight is a great promoter. The Jack Dempsey–Jess Willard fight was the brainchild of a brilliant and cunning entrepreneur, Tex Rickard. He was the first in a short list of boxing promoters who had both vision and financial daring. Rickard was also the first to understand the value of prefight hoopla and press coverage.

For a few years Rickard had had his eye on Dempsey, who was from Manassa, Colorado, and was known as the Manassa Mauler, as a challenger for Jess Willard, the 6-foot-6-inch heavyweight champion nicknamed the Pottawatomie Giant, after his hometown in Kansas. Willard, 37, an easygoing, amiable gent, had become a big favorite in America after taking the title from the roundly despised black champion, Jack Johnson, whose insistence on racial equality made him unpopular among many white fans. In Rickard's scheme for a big, crowd-pleasing bout, Willard was the "white hat."

And in Dempsey the promoter had a "black hat." The charge that he had dodged the draft was held against Dempsey in postwar America, and everywhere he went, crowds scorned the 24-year-old brawler as a "slacker." The formula for a box-office success—bad guy vs. good guy—was insured. The final element to be put in place was financing, which in turn would dictate location.

If there was anything Tex Rickard was the master of, it was the Big Con. He decided to hold this jewel of a heavyweight championship match in Toledo, Ohio, on July 4, 1919—Independence Day, the perfect occasion for local patriots to vent their hatred of Dempsey. The proposed bout proved controversial, however, with Ohio Governor James M. Cox its principal opponent. When Cox banned the fight, the reckless Rickard offered him a $25,000 bribe, which infuriated the governor. In high dudgeon, Cox protested to reporters, "Rickard can't buy me for $25,000." Unruffled, the brash promoter responded, "Hell, I didn't want to buy him. I just wanted to rent him for an afternoon." The storm eventually passed, and permission was granted for the fight to proceed.

MAULER VS. GIANT

The indispensable ingredients of a great fight are the fighters and their competing characteristics. In the case of Dempsey-Willard, fight fans were presented with a most intriguing matchup: Good vs. Evil, Patriot vs. Slacker, Young vs. Old, Big vs. Small, Meritorious Champion vs. Questionably Virtuous Challenger.

At age 24, Dempsey had already led a checkered life. On his own since he was 13, he vagabonded across the Rocky Mountain states, working as a carnival fighter, mule driver, and professional pool shark. Dempsey used his tremendous punching power to make extra cash by sauntering into local saloons and betting he could "beat any man in the house." Considering that Dempsey had weighed only 130 pounds as a teenager, he must have packed a dynamite punch, although he concedes in his autobiography, "I got flattened now and then."

Dempsey was as much a hustler as he was a professional boxer. He rarely trained, and he would throw a fight for the right price. On one such low occasion he accepted $300 to take a dive for Fireman Joe Flynn, a famous heavyweight. Dempsey splashed down in the first round. Later, embarrassed by his staged collapse, he challenged Flynn to a rematch. This time, in a legitimate fight, Dempsey knocked out a surprised Fireman Joe in one round.

With the exception of Cassius Clay (later known worldwide, of course, as Muhammad Ali) and a handful of others, great fighters are infrequently born great. Most are the product of their managers and trainers. In this respect Jack Dempsey lucked out. By a serendipitous turn of events, he stumbled into the company of a fabulous con artist named Jack "Doc" Kearns. Doc had occasionally dabbled in prizefighting, and when he laid eyes on the lean, mean, ferocious young Dempsey, he agreed to manage and train him as a "favor": Dempsey would owe Kearns nothing for his contracted services, but would pay him 50 percent of the boxer's earnings throughout his lifetime. In signing on with Kearns, Dempsey had made both the best and the worst move of his young life.

Kearns understood that Dempsey was "right-hand crazy," and that his only defense was his relentless offense. He took Dempsey to a gym and tied his right arm to his body, forcing the fighter to spar with skilled heavyweights using only his left hand. Kearns also insisted that Dempsey spar entire rounds only on defense, thus teaching him to bob and weave, crouch, and otherwise move his head to avoid punches. This was the making of one of the fiercest fighting machines in the history of boxing.

Doc Kearns's one mistake came with the nation's entry into World War I. American boys flocked to join the armed forces. Dempsey was eager to go, but Kearns filed for a deferment from military service, on the grounds that Dempsey was the sole support of his wife, Maxine, whom he described as a part-time piano player. The couple soon split up, however, and Maxine confessed to the press that she was actually a prostitute.

To put out the fire that this revelation ignited, Kearns launched a PR campaign in which Jack made morale-boosting visits to army training camps and defense plants. A photograph from one of these visits backfired seriously on the boxer, however. The photo showed a young, muscular Dempsey, his sleeves rolled up, wearing a long workman's apron and holding a riveting machine while standing next to a real riveter in a similar pose. The trouble lay at the bottom of the picture: rather than wearing scuffed work boots, as might be expected, Dempsey was sporting patent leather street shoes with white spats. The public outcry of derision was deafening.

After a year of fighting all over the country, under Kearns's masterful guidance, Dempsey was ready for his part in Tex Rickard's plan to pit the Manassa Mauler against the Pottawatomie Giant. But with the bout all set for July 4, 1919, in Toledo, Doc Kearns made the first of two uncharacteristically ill-advised moves.

In the first blunder, Tex Rickard offered Doc a percentage of the gate rather than a flat fee of $27,500. Doc sneered at Tex's offer and took the $27,500 instead. In hindsight this choice was laughably bad, as Kearns's percentage of the gate would have totaled $200,000. Doc's second mistake was betting $10,000, at 10-to-1 odds, that Dempsey would win the fight in the first round.

Jess Willard was the prototype of an unbeatable world heavyweight champion. At age 37 he was a full 6 feet 6 inches tall, weighed 250 pounds, had an eaglelike arm span of 83 inches, and—best of all for the American public of that era—was as white as the driven snow. A sane, sober, family man, Jess had no ghosts in his closet. He was the textbook "good guy."

Willard had found his place in America's heart by beating the "villainous" Jack Johnson, the first black man to hold the heavyweight title. Johnson had enraged the Caucasian public with his "uppity" ways, capping a series of amorous adventures with white women by marrying one of them. Boxing fans embraced Willard, issuing a mandate for him to "flatten Jack Johnson."

On a very hot April 5, 1915, in Havana, Cuba, Willard complied, administering a convincing thrashing of Johnson over 26 rounds. Willard went into training confident that he could beat the relatively tiny Dempsey, who stood just over 6 feet tall, weighed little more than 180 pounds, and had a short reach—meager credentials for a heavyweight contender. Willard began to count in advance his $100,000 purse and look forward to a pleasant Fourth of July celebration after the fight.

The bookmaking establishment, however, taking note of Dempsey's determined training regimen and hunger for victory and the acceptance it would bring, made Dempsey a narrow favorite, at odds of 10 to 8. The stage was set for a memorable battle.

THE SHOWDOWN

Forty thousand hardy souls arrived early at the Toledo Arena, in anticipation of the great event. Most of the men were in shirtsleeves and wore straw boaters to protect their heads from the broiling summer sun. Surprisingly, 500 women were also in attendance, parasols in hand; a testament to the widespread attractiveness of the fight. In the overheated arena, the July sun caused resin to boil and seep from the freshly cut wooden seats. The public laid newspapers and handkerchiefs on the lumber to shield their skin and clothing from both heat and resin. By fight time the temperature had soared to 114 degrees at ringside.

The fighters entered the ring, Dempsey to boos and cries of "slacker!" and Willard to rousing cheers. The referee, Ollie Pecord, delivered the preliminary instructions and the fighters repaired to their corners to await the opening bell.

There followed a series of events that affected the outcome of the fight and caused Doc Kearns to lose his bet on a first-round victory by Dempsey.

Before the main event commenced, a contingent of marines entered the ring and performed a demonstration of a close-order drill. The significant effect of this impressive bit of marching was

As Dempsey entered the ring in Toledo, his wrapped left hand offered no evidence to support his manager's subsequent claim of an illegal substance in the fighter's gloves. (*The Robert Shepard Collection*)

to scuff and wrinkle the ring canvas, requiring its replacement with a new one. In their haste to stretch and fix the new canvas in place, the workers nailed it down—over the bell! There would be no bell to announce the beginning and end of each round. One of the boxing commissioners present, Warren Barbour, issued a police whistle to do the job of the bell. This substitution would be a pivotal factor in the outcome of the fight. As it happened, the start of the bout was delayed 10 seconds while both boxers waited in their corners for the familiar bell to sound, having failed to hear the whistle that was blown. Had the fight started when the whistle blew, Willard would have been knocked out in one round and Dempsey and Kearns would have won $100,000—the equivalent of about $1.5 million today—on Doc's wager.

The whistle finally blew, starting the first round. In Dempsey's corner the volatile Kearns held his fighter back for a moment and whispered in his ear, "I've bet $10,000 that you'll knock him out in the first round." This added an instant turbocharge to Dempsey's motor. Racing across the ring, Dempsey confronted a complacent Pottawatomie Giant, who was expecting a stroll in the park against an undersized opponent.

The first thing that struck fans was the fighters' disparity in size. Willard was colossal, towering over Dempsey, who, fully half a foot shorter, was lean and deeply suntanned, resembling a sleek panther. From the outset it was evident that a new era in boxing had arrived. A crouching Dempsey, his gloves held low, bobbed and weaved his way around the ring, in stark contrast to the ramrod-straight Willard, who held his hands high in the old-fashioned style of Gentleman Jim Corbett.

The first 85 or 90 seconds went by peacefully enough, as Dempsey circled the plodding Willard, throwing a weak left jab from time to time. His right hand was cocked, ready to attack the champ's body. With Dempsey in a stealthy crouch and the giant Willard standing upright, the latter's pale body offered an inviting target. In time Dempsey landed the fight's first solid, meaningful punch, a beauty of a right hand under the heart. Willard's face registered its effect.

Willard reflexively put out his long arms and wrapped them around Dempsey, who seized the advantage, driving lefts and

rights to the champion's soft belly. Referee Pecord did not inter-
fere as the fighters repeatedly clinched and Dempsey pounded
Willard's ribs. Willard winced as his rib cage gradually caved in
under the force of the blows.

Suddenly, Dempsey uncoiled from his crouch and landed several
solid left hands, saving his killer right hand for a closer. When it
came, it landed with imposing force. Willard blinked, and before he
could relax, Dempsey administered his coup de grace, a zinging left
hook. Willard sagged, staggered to the ropes, and crumpled as
Dempsey rained down a storm of rights and lefts.

With one minute left in the first round, the ref, Pecord, began
his count, as Dempsey hovered over his fallen adversary. Willard,
using the rope, tried to get up, but as soon as his knee left the
canvas, the waiting Dempsey pummeled him with lethal combinations. Willard collapsed again, knocked down for a second
time. The ref struggled to remove Dempsey from the vicinity so
he could begin the count, but Dempsey stayed within punching
range. Willard pulled himself upright on the ropes, only to
receive another barrage of vicious lefts and rights. Down went
Willard, for the third time in the round.

As Willard lifted himself yet again, his body nearly doubled over,
facing the canvas, Dempsey displayed his homicidal bent. With devastating force he landed an overhand right to the back of Willard's
head. This was an illegal and clearly dangerous punch, but for some
reason Pecord chose to ignore it. The blow sent Willard once more
onto the canvas. This was the fourth knockdown he had suffered.
How much more could the giant take?

Somehow Willard rose again, only to be dropped for a fifth
time by a punishing flurry of Dempsey punches. One side of the
champion's face was now swollen to nearly twice its normal size,
a sure sign of fractured facial bones. One of his eyes was closed,
and blood spurted from his nose. Knockdown number five
should have been more than enough to finish him off, but a stoppage of the fight deemed premature by the crowd would have
netted Pecord a hanging. Slowly, incredibly, Willard rose again.

This time the battered champ managed to vacate the spot of

the multiple knockdowns and lurch across the ring, his back to his pursuing opponent. Dempsey fired a strong right hand that landed on the back of Willard's neck, near the base of his skull. The giant toppled over, his arm hooked on the middle rope. Dempsey continued punching even though Willard was clearly down again. The ref got between the fighters and, for the sixth time in the round, began his count. Willard's face was a grotesque bloody mask. His skin was splotched and lumped with blue-black knots. He was a thoroughly beaten fighter.

Yet, to the profound astonishment of 40,000 screaming fans, Willard painfully and heroically pulled himself up on the ropes. Dempsey once again was waiting for him. The seventh knockdown came mercifully fast. Like an imploding building, Willard collapsed one story at a time. When he did not get back up, pandemonium broke out. Fans seated at ringside rushed to help Willard. Dempsey went to a neutral corner. An ebullient Doc Kearns raced over and put a towel over Dempsey's shoulders, instructing him to rush to the dressing room and take a shower. Dempsey was halfway out of the auditorium when Kearns frantically waved him back in. The whistle had been blown, ending the round and saving (if that's the right word) Willard. This fight was not yet over, and therein lay the kernel of a controversy.

Things might have turned out differently had a wily, resourceful manager like Doc Kearns been in Willard's corner. A savvy cornerman could have demanded that the whistle be blown to start Round 2, and that Dempsey be disqualified because he was out of the ring at the start of the round. Willard would have retained his title while sitting, bloodied and dazed, on his stool. But, notes the writer Roger Kahn, "Willard was a tightwad. He didn't want to spend money to hire professional cornermen. It cost him the championship."

To everyone's amazement, the bout continued. Dempsey had nearly punched himself out by now, so the inevitable outcome was postponed for two more long and agonizing rounds. The end came when Willard failed to answer the whistle for Round 4.

THE UNTOLD STORY

Now the real controversy arose. How could Dempsey have inflicted the damage that Willard absorbed without a little help in his gloves?

The damage was indeed severe. In the first round Willard's zygomatic arch (cheekbone) was broken in 12 places. In the same round the champion sustained a broken nose, a jaw that was broken in 13 places, and eight avulsed teeth. In addition to facial fractures, he suffered two fractured ribs. Reports of his injuries varied, and the use of X-rays was primitive at the time, but any way you cut it, an enormous amount of damage was produced in a single round.

For his part, Willard maintained that crime figures were behind his brutal defeat. "The gamblers and the gangsters took my title away from me," he said later. "I could beat any prizefighter, but I can't beat gangsters, and that is exactly what I was up against." Doc Kearns spun a variety of tales, pleading total innocence one day and the next admitting, with a wink, to having placed plaster of paris in Dempsey's glove. Indeed, Kearns sold his plaster of paris story to a sports magazine, but the tale was quickly disproved. Dempsey always insisted that the fight was totally aboveboard. That was his story, and he stuck to it throughout his life.

Referee Pecord starts the count as the Manassa Mauler circles the fallen Willard. (*Hank Kaplan Archives*)

It remained for Doc to come up with a strange and fascinating wrinkle, and by luck I happened to be one of several sportswriters and boxing insiders in whom Doc confided. We were staying at the Alexandria Hotel in Los Angeles. I was working with Luis Manuel Rodriguez, who was about to fight Emile Griffith for the welterweight title in Chavez Ravine. It was March 1963, and Doc Kearns joined us every morning for breakfast and a round of boxing stories. As it turned out, Doc had only a short time left to live. He died on July 8 of that year.

One morning Doc showed up with an 8 mm movie projector and a reel of film from the Dempsey-Willard fight. "I got a big surprise for you wise guys," he said, the twinkle in his eye tipping off that he had something startling to show us.

His running commentary was hilarious, but he got quiet when Round 1 ended. Apparently, the fight was over. On the screen, the crowd surged forward to assist the battered Willard. Dempsey was left alone. Neither his seconds nor Doc rushed to celebrate, as Dempsey walked to a neutral corner. Dempsey dropped his hand by his side, and out came an iron object that resembled a railroad spike.

There was a rustle in the hotel room. We couldn't accept the evidence before our eyes. "Hell, ol' Doc must have doctored the tape, painted that iron spike in frame by frame," someone mused aloud. Doc froze the film's frame at that point, enjoying our wise-guy doubts.

"And now, gentlemen, the proof that this film is authentic: keep your eyes on the spike."

The film started up again, and we saw a man, who had been seated by the ring, take off his hat and place it over the spike. The man paused, looked around, then reached under his hat. He picked up the hat and grabbed the spike, then put the spike in his pocket. At that point Dempsey moved into Doc's waiting embrace.

I have never seen that piece of film again. The men who were with me in that room—the respected writers Bob Waters, Jim Murray, Shirley Povich, and Lester Bromberg, along with a few boxing reporters from the West Coast—are all dead now. Doc's son claims never to have seen that reel of film. It's as if Doc's secret died with him.

Doc was such a canny old sorcerer and yarn spinner that none of us present could believe what we had seen with our own eyes. That piece of film from 1919 must have been forged or altered. Such was Doc's reputation that we doubted the veracity of what was right in front of us. In fact, evidence suggests that a venegeful Jess Willard, unable to accept the devastation that Dempsey had wreaked upon him, did forge the film, with help from his brother.

I've been a physician in boxing for almost 40 years, and I have never seen such anatomical damage as Jack Dempsey inflicted on Jess Willard. Even in the days of bare-knuckle fighting, there is no record of such extensive facial carnage as Willard incurred. To shatter a cheekbone 12 times, you'd have to hit it with a ball-peen hammer. What gave Dempsey such power? Why didn't the bones in his own hands break under the force of his punches?

Roger Kahn, the noted sportswriter, is the author of *A Flame of Pure Fire*, a fine book covering the Dempsey-Willard bout, and a ranking authority on Dempsey and his career. Kahn rejects the notion that Dempsey was assisted by a spike or other foreign substance in or outside of his gloves. Nevertheless, Kahn's insights on Dempsey are provocative.

"Dempsey was fighting with terror in his heart," says Kahn. "He certainly had a motive—the bet, and the fear that Willard might recover and attack him—to do whatever it took to win. Could he have inflicted that much damage? Sure he could have. Was that a spike or a gefilte fish in his glove? We're not sure. Willard, for the rest of his life, would point to a dent in his facial bone and say, 'Nobody could dent my bone like that.' Willard went to his grave convinced that he was 'jobbed' by a crooked fighter—or so he said.

"I would rather think it was not an iron spike, but we have to remember where it was in the early part of the century that Dempsey came from: a very, very tough America," Kahn continues. "When he was traveling in boxcars, he had to fight for his life against homosexual rape. His first wife was a prostitute, and he was her pimp. He was accused of many things, including being a professional rapist of virgins who would then be sent to brothels. Some of this is undoubtedly so. It was a very tough America, and Dempsey did what he had to do to win."

And where do I stand? With the King of Siam, who simply said, "Is a puzzlement."

Down for the Long Count: With Tunney on the canvas, referee Barry points Dempsey toward a neutral corner in the seventh round of one of boxing's most memorable bouts. (*Corbis/Bettmann–UPI*)

THE LONG COUNT

JACK DEMPSEY   vs.   GENE TUNNEY
CHALLENGER   CHAMPION

HEAVYWEIGHT CHAMPIONSHIP
SEPTEMBER 22, 1927
CHICAGO

ROUND 7

Following the bloodbath of the First World War and a nationwide flu epidemic, American society returned to its carefree ways. The public took to the roads as the automobile became an increasingly affordable commodity and highways were built apace. The Jazz Age arrived on a heady cloud of bootleg booze and hot music. America was one big party town.

Amid the general prosperity sports were as popular as ever, and many of the biggest sports events were world championship boxing matches. For hundreds of young men, many of them from newly arrived immigrant families, boxing was a passport out of poverty and possibly into affluence. Every town had a local boxing club and its local-favorite boxer.

The enactment of Prohibition briefly cast a pall on all the fun, but the widely unpopular law soon gave rise to new ways to make a buck. It also spawned a new kind of criminal, the gangster. It turned out that gangsters, just like their upstanding fellow citizens, had "favorite" boxers too, but in a slightly different sense.

It was a golden era for sports. Boxing, as it often did, provided a champion for the decade. Jack Dempsey was white, fearsome, and in most ways a PR man's dream. Nearly everybody loved him. He had married a beautiful movie star, Estelle Taylor, and was a man-about-town on two coasts.

Due to acrimonious disputes with his irascible manager, Doc Kearns, and his satisfaction with the glamorous high life, Dempsey did not fight in 1924 and 1925. He waited almost another year before deciding to risk his crown against an ex-marine and New York City native named Gene Tunney.

Tunney was movie-star handsome, highly intelligent, and a student of the art of boxing. Weighing as little as 155 pounds early in his career, he was considered too light to be an effective heavyweight, however. His lack of heft, coupled with a light punch, seemed to make him an ideal opponent for the heavy-fisted Dempsey. A bout between the two men was set for the fall of 1926.

Dempsey, taking stock of his condition after a prolonged lay-off from fighting and some sustained partygoing, insisted that the fight be limited to 10 rounds instead of the standard 15. He knew he would feel the effects of ring rust, and at age 31 he was two years older than his opponent. The decision to make it a 10-rounder delighted Tunney, who planned to stay as far away as possible from Dempsey throughout the fight. For Tunney, it would be a lot easier to run for 10 rounds than for 15.

On the appointed date—September 23, 1926— before a crowd of 120,757 fans at Philadelphia's Sesquicentennial Stadium, Tunney worked his plan to perfection, dancing deftly away from the huffing, puffing Dempsey for 10 rounds. When the decision was announced, Gene Tunney was the new world heavyweight champion. But he was less than popular among boxing fans, who felt betrayed. Why, they asked, hadn't the young marine stood his ground and fought like a man, instead of running out of harm's way?

Meanwhile, for the first time since the Willard fight, Jack Dempsey left a boxing arena to cheers rather than boos. He may have looked a bit past his prime, but at least he had been willing to slug it out with the elusive Tunney. "They boo me when I win, and I had to lose to get them to cheer me," Dempsey, a gracious loser, said in the dressing room after the fight. Outside that room, Tex Rickard began licking his chops. A rematch would break all box-office records, and the stage was soon set for Dempsey-Tunney, Part 2.

THE FIGHT

On a hot September 22 night in 1927 at Soldier Field in Chicago, 104,943 eager fight fans gathered to see Jack Dempsey beat up Gene Tunney and regain the heavyweight crown that was rightfully his and, in the process, gain a sweet, satisfying measure of revenge.

Ticket sales yielded a record gate of $2,658,660, enabling Tex Rickard to make Tunney history's first boxer to earn a million dollars for a single fight. Dempsey got $450,000, of which Doc Kearns took his customary half. The betting opened and closed with Tunney a 7-to-5 favorite, but the crowd was solidly behind the ex-champ.

In the early going the two boxers took up where they had left off, Dempsey stalking and Tunney throwing sharp jabs to Dempsey's face. Tunney was ahead on all scorecards by the end of the sixth round, but at the start of the seventh, Dempsey caught Tunney flush on the jaw and the former marine's legs buckled.

With Tunney dazed and vulnerable, the old fury of the Manassa Mauler was unleashed. Like a bolt of lightning, Dempsey flashed punishing lefts and rights, each packed with all of the fighter's considerable power. Tunney was folding, trying feebly to ward off the punches, but Dempsey kept swarming. Dempsey landed a low body shot, then a hard blow to the back of the head as Tunney turned away from the challenger's fury.

Tunney went down, his knees meeting the canvas at a spot near the ropes, but Dempsey—the onetime fierce panther of the mining camps, the destroyer of gigantic Jess Willard—would not stop punching. The referee, Dave Barry, tried to get a grip on the windmilling Dempsey and pull him off his wounded opponent.

This effort cost precious seconds—lost time when Barry should have been counting over the fallen Tunney. Dempsey hovered behind the ref, who refused to start the count until Dempsey went to a neutral corner as required by a new rule. The new rule was in effect, but in Dempsey's excited mind he was still fighting by the old rules, the rules of boxcars and barrooms.

Tunney later recalled the events of that seventh round. "Everybody saw Dempsey land that left hook to my jaw, but never knew how much it surprised me," he said. "I never saw the punch. Not seeing it coming surprised me—I was always cocksure about my eyesight in the ring. The blow was the second of a series of seven that put me on the canvas for the first time in my life. I remember clearly Dempsey crossing a vicious right over my left lead for the first punch of that series. I scolded myself for being hit by such an obvious blow. What I said to myself was, 'Tunney, what a sucker you are to be nailed by that.' The next cerebration was that I'd been hit a helluva shot on the right jaw. I hadn't seen the wallop start or in flight, but I certainly felt it. It was the hardest of the seven and the one that prepared me for the five others, and the much-discussed and unpleasant 14 seconds' rest on the canvas."

From that quote one can deduce that Tunney was an unusually alert fighter with great powers of observation, a good vocabulary, and an aptitude for putting into words an event that took but seconds to occur. If you think he was unusually expressive for a fighter, listen to his semi-alibi, which offers even more supportive evidence.

"My blindness to the melodramatic punch was caused, I conscientiously believe, by a traumatic astigmatism due to a severe eye injury sustained in training. I got thumbed and the blood vessels leading to the retina were damaged. Two Chicago specialists rushed to the camp and began treatment, and then I began to see a little out of the injured right eye, and it was one of the great moments of my life. I was not going to lose the sight of my right eye! This is not to be construed in any way as an alibi."

Had he lost the fight, you'd have heard a lot more about the eye, but winning fighters can afford to be magnanimous.

THE COUNT: HOW LONG?

Back in the ring, Tunney is on the floor. Dempsey is looming over him. Referee Barry is pointing to a neutral corner, trying to steer Dempsey in that direction so he can begin the count. Finally, Dempsey comes to his senses as his corner screams at him to move. The ref raises his arm and begins to count. Tunney, still in a seated position on the floor, reaches for the rope with one arm. Barry has started counting: "One . . . two . . ."

Dempsey was quoted as follows in the *New York Times*.

"When the bell started us on the seventh round, I went out for a do-or-die round. I wanted to surprise Gene. After a minute of the routine body attack, I suddenly straightened and let fly a right to the jaw. It landed as I hoped and planned and it sure was a beaut. I had plenty of hop on it, and it staggered Gene back on his heels.

"Just how badly he was hurt only Gene knows. I let loose a left hook he didn't see. Even if he had three eyes he couldn't have seen that punch coming, because he was in a position on the ropes where he couldn't very well do anything."

Dempsey continued: "I saw I had him. Then I let loose with everything I had and poured leather into him until he sank like an empty meal sack to the floor of the ring. I knew he was 'out.' And I was nearly so myself. But I felt that I had finished the job, and with everything all over, I let down and relaxed. I felt that so far as I was concerned, I had carried out my plan exactly as I had mapped it out. But, I was wrong. Tunney got back up, recovered and my luck ran out.

"Maybe I was lucky, after all. I am perfectly willing to accept the ruling on the Long Count. I do know this. If there was actually a long count, it was a good thing for me. I had absorbed a terrible beating in both fights around my eyes. Had

I won that second fight, there would have had to be a third fight—and I might not be able to see today!"

Upon subsequently viewing the film of the fight, Dempsey commented, "I don't know or care how long Gene was down. I was pretty doggone tired myself. Paul Beeler, the timekeeper, later explained that he was leaning on the edge of the ring, holding his stopwatch in his left hand. On his table were two more stopwatches, left running to record the time for starting and stopping the rounds.

"The round was just 50 seconds old when I started my attack. We were a few feet from my corner. Gene was careless as the round started and wasn't carrying his hands as high as he should have. Suddenly, I exploded on his chin. Every punch connected. Beeler said he jumped to his feet, ready to start the count, when Gene went down. Beeler said he started the count when Tunney's hips hit the

Tunney turned the tables in Round 8, decking Dempsey en route to a 10-round decision. (*Corbis/Bettmann–UPI*)

floor. He reached the count of five, he said, when he couldn't hear the ref's voice counting with him and he glanced up."

Here is what Paul Beeler recalls. "Two things flashed into my vision," said the timekeeper. "Barry faced me and was swinging his right hand, yelling out the count, *one*. I had a split second in which to decide whether to go with Barry's count or continue my own original count, which had started when Tunney was floored. I went along with referee Barry; he was in charge. When Barry reached the count of nine, Tunney got to his feet and did a great job of backpedaling for the rest of the round. My watch read 17 seconds! Why 17 seconds? Well, Barry had inadvertently slowed down the cadence of the count from five to nine. Why was a count of 14 reported? That was due to the sportswriters' adding my five seconds to Barry's nine count."

In actuality, then, as much as 17 seconds had elapsed. How could this have happened?

Beeler explained, "It's difficult to count seconds accurately without using a stopwatch, the general tendency being to count them slower than they actually are. That's what referee Barry did."

So, had the count been timed correctly—that is, according to the timekeeper's stopwatch—the outcome would have been a Dempsey victory. Instead, as boxing fans know, Gene Tunney, rescued by the Long Count of Round 7, went on to win a 10-round decision over Dempsey and retain his heavyweight title. For Dempsey it was the end of the road. The Manassa Mauler never fought again, announcing his retirement on March 4, 1928.

Clues to what transpired in that seventh round can be gleaned from the film of the fight. It should be noted that film from this era runs faster than "real" time, due to the newsreel technology of the day. It is therefore difficult to get an accurate count of Tunney's time on the canvas based on the film footage. As Roger Kahn points out, however, this piece of film has been inspected closely.

"Right after the fight, [boxer and future referee] Benny Leonard and Hype Igoe, a very good newswriter of his day, got the film. Using sprockets and stopwatches, they timed it and timed it, over and over again. It took them two weeks to put together their report for the *New York World*. And they concluded that Tunney was on the canvas for 17 or 18 seconds," says Kahn.

"The question is not only whether Tunney could have gotten up. If he had gotten up he would have been confused, and if you're confused in the ring with Jack Dempsey, it's all over."

THE UNTOLD STORY

Right at this point is where the background, the untold story, gets murky. The main culprit seems to be the referee, Dave Barry. Who was he? Why was he hired to work this important fight? Did he affect the outcome? Was he crooked? Was the fix in?

And what about Gene Tunney? Superficially, at least, he was an impressive, virtuous fellow, squeaky clean and intellectual. But did the substance match the surface?

In my interview with Roger Kahn, the writer disclosed that referee Barry had some skeletons in his closet, while Tunney's background included an unsavory relationship with organized crime.

"For a start," says Kahn, "we have Gene Tunney involved with the Philadelphia mob headed by 'Boo Boo' Hoff and his pals. Boo Boo was an ominous figure in those days. Al Capone in Chicago admired boxers, so he wanted to manage Dempsey, who had the common sense to decline Al's offer. Capone did not get mad, and remained heavily committed to Dempsey.

"Two referees were considered for the fight. Dave Miller, whom Benny Leonard considered the best in the country, was favored for the assignment. Word filtered down to Philly that Capone liked Miller, and that Capone was trying to fix the fight. At this point a second ref is mentioned: Dave Barry. Now, Barry is running a speakeasy in Chicago; this is something that Capone does not like, but anyway, the fact is that Dave Barry is operating outside the law.

"Where but in Chicago in the twenties," Kahn concludes, "could you have a hoodlum referee a world title fight."

The Long Count has been analyzed in every possible way. What has been overlooked, however, is Dave Barry's behavior in the next round, the eighth, when Tunney knocks Dempsey down. Where is Barry at that time? Right on top of Dempsey, counting "One . . . " as soon as Dempsey's rear end hits the canvas. And Tunney? Did he run to a neutral corner so that Barry could begin the count? Hardly, says Kahn: "Tunney was as close to a neutral corner as I am to Moscow. And this was not the only evidence of a biased ref. A referee has many ways to influence a fight; for example, on the break."

One of Dempsey's favorite tactics was to hit on the break—as he was moving back out of a clinch, he'd pull the other fighter with one hand and sucker punch him with the other. Dempsey was fierce coming out of a clinch. He won an important fight with ex-champ Jack Sharkey by using his wits. Sharkey, hit low by Dempsey, turned to the ref in a clinch to complain, and Dempsey decked him. When criticized for hitting on the break, Dempsey deadpanned, 'What was I suppose to do, send him a letter?'"

In this fight, Dave Barry would grab Dempsey's right arm so that he could not punch or move the other fighter, in effect neutralizing Dempsey's infighting.

All of these factors, along with the fact that Boo Boo Hoff had loaned Tunney a staggering $200,000, gave the fight its lingering piscine aroma. Tunney was no saint, and neither was Dempsey. Tunney never did explain his connection with Boo Boo Hoff. He didn't need to; there was no postfight investigation.

HOW I SEE IT

Looking at the film today, studying it in slow motion, I have to conclude that if the injured Gene Tunney had gotten up at a legitimate eight count, he would clearly have been knocked out. No one could survive Jack Dempsey's fury when he had an opponent in trouble.

The seven successive hard punches thrown by Dempsey were designed to hurt every part of Tunney. The barrage included a shot to the jaw, digging punches to his ribs and midsection, and a "Dempsey Special"—a rabbit punch to the back of the head, which today is illegal. Dempsey made his reputation by finishing big, finishing with finality, as he had in mining-camp slugfests: raining punches to every quarter until the other fighter was supine. On this occasion Dempsey kept working until Tunney keeled over. How Tunney got up after what may have been 17 seconds can only be attributed to the former marine's youth, conditioning, and heart.

Even so, Tunney's boxing smarts and young legs alone might not explain his resiliency. I look at Tunney's escape differently— as an indication that the great, ferocious Jack Dempsey was no more. He was a shot, spent fighter, but no one wanted to say it.

Conversations I had with wily old Abe Attell, a onetime featherweight champion and a member of the International Boxing Hall of Fame, shed light on both of the Dempsey-Tunney fights. Abe, who died at age 85 in 1970, was deeply involved in New York boxing, and also in the underworld in New York and beyond. The mob has always been a familiar presence on the boxing scene.

I spent many long hours at New York watering holes such as Toots Shor's and the Friars Club, and in gyms, listening to hundreds of Abe's boxing stories from 1910 on. As a fighter Abe had been a big fan favorite, offering the unusual combination of being both Jewish and a magnificent boxer. He was particularly popular with Jewish clothiers who liked to place a bet. Abe had the ability to "carry" an opponent to a specific round, then knock him out. He would share such plans with the clothiers. He had an alternative "safe bet," too: the "distance" bet, whereby he would tell the his wagering pals in advance whether the fight would go the distance. Employing such tactics, Abe made a fortune.

Hearing that I was injecting Muhammad Ali's hands before each fight with Novocain, Abe cornered me at Toots Shor's one day and told me the following story.

"I had a big fight coming up in Madison Square Garden, but I hurt my hands punching the bag. I couldn't call the fight off. My bettors had bet me to win, big. I was the favorite, and I shoulda been. I was much better than the other mug. The morning of the fight my hands hurt like hell. One of my millionaire clothiers shows up at my apartment as I was gettin' ready to go to the fight. He has a gent with a black bag. He introduces him as Dr. Flynn, his plastic surgeon, and he tells me he is going to numb my hands. He gets in the car and we go to the Garden.

"Now, this is around 1918 or so, and no one ever heard of doctors in boxing. So we goes in the toilet stall and he shoots up my hands. Well, I coulda hit George M. Cohan's statue and done damage. I was set.

"But that night wasn't my night! I couldn't catch the bum to hit him. I'd hoped the wise guys had heard I had bum dukes, and the pug would come to me, but that wasn't for him. He out-boxes me good. I lose the decision! Big trouble from the guys that laid the price on Abe Attell to win, and the other guys that laid the price that I was knocking out the bum! Everyone thought I'd bet the short side, me as the underdog, and thrown it.

"That night I get death threats from a few of the 'boys' that has got well-deserved reputations for professional excellence. I hadda do something!

"So I calls the New York papers—the *Post*, the *Brooklyn Eagle*, all of 'em—and give 'em the story that I was doped by the plastic surgeon, Flynn, and I'm going to the boxing commission to place a charge against him and get the match called a no-contest.

"There was a big hoo-ha, but the boys believed my story even if the commission said it would have nothing to do with a no-contest ruling. I guess they had a few bucks on my opponent. Anyway, I survived!"

The clincher to that story happened 20 years after Abe told me his tale. While attending a plastic surgery conference in Miami, I ran into none other than the now ancient Dr. Flynn. He confirmed the story exactly as Abe Attell had related it to me that night at Toots Shor's. Flynn added that he had never had anything to do with boxing thereafter.

Abe was a mother lode of information on the second Dempsey-Tunney fight, having been a dark part of the first. Dempsey has charged that Attell, in concert with the mobster Arnie Rothstein (who fixed the 1919 "Black Sox" World Series) was working with Tunney associates to appoint a "friendly" referee, fix the size of the ring, and change the rules, specifically, the neutral-corner rule. This scenario is at least plausible, since it turns out that the $200,000 Tunney had borrowed came not only from the Philly hood Boo Boo Hoff, but also from Abe Attell.

The involvement of mobsters was a factor in nearly every major fight in the twenties. Mob guys were inherently drawn to the tough world of boxing, and they had yet to figure out that their involvement with a boxer drew the spotlight to them, too. In the case of Al Capone, the spotlight revealed a white Borsalino hat, a big cigar, and a cashmere coat, all of which piqued the curiosity of the Internal Revenue Service with regard to Capone's business records. Eventually, after the fifties, gangsters knew better than to appear next to a champion in a boxing arena.

But until then they did little to conceal their relationships with fighters, and vice versa, as Abe Attell demonstrates in his stories about the Dempsey-Tunney rivalry.

"In those days the mob boys took over cities as their territory. The Italians had Chicago; the Jews had Philly and some parts of Detroit," said Abe.

"Capone loved Dempsey. Jack Dempsey was way bigger than Capone, and didn't need him. In fact, he was an embarrassment. Still, it didn't hurt none that Capone was 'interested' in Dempsey not getting screwed.

"Tunney, who was a real authentic gentleman and an ex-marine, had a similar situation in Philly with Boo Boo Hoff, but he made the mistake of borrowing money from Boo Boo, so the connection was tighter than Dempsey with Capone.

"Now, if Jack had not been on the outs with Doc Kearns, none of the trouble that happened woulda happened. But they wasn't talking. Doc had robbed him blind, and Dempsey had had enough. The way Dempsey saw it, Kearns mistook gratitude for stupidity."

Abe leaned in close to me, whispering the way mob guys do when they want to share a secret with you. "What you had was this, Doc: It was the Italians against the Jews. The Jews won!" He shrugged his shoulders as if the result was obvious. The Jews, in this case, meant Tunney, through his connection to the Jewish-controlled Philly mob.

"Look what they got from the Illinois Boxing Commission for the first fight. Kearns always insisted on a 16-foot ring when Dempsey fought. In a phone booth nobody walks out alive but Dempsey. Somehow, though, Tunney ended up with a 20-footer for this fight—a ring made for a track meet.

"For the second fight, the rematch in Chicago, the most important thing they got—pay attention here—was a ref, Dave Barry, who made up the rules to help Tunney. If he had his way, Kearns would not have allowed Barry to be the ref or allowed the new neutral-corner rule or the big ring size; none of it. Every corner is neutral until the bell rings to stop the contest, was Kearns's view. But unfortunately, Dempsey did not have Doc Kearns to maneuver for him, since they were on the outs."

In the matter of the Long Count, an interesting scenario occurs featuring the referee, Dave Barry. As we've seen, when Tunney went down in Round 7 he received a slow count, which, observers agree today, lasted 14 to 17 seconds.

The fight continued, and when early in the eighth round Tunney knocked Dempsey down, referee Barry sprang forward and promptly started the count: "One . . ." The fact is, however, that Tunney had not yet started to move to a neutral corner. He was lurking behind the referee, just as Dempsey had done in the previous round! Apparently, Dave Barry now applied a different set of rules for Tunney!

But what's done is irrevocably done. Two things happened on that memorable September night in Chicago: Gene Tunney walked away from the ring with his heavyweight crown intact, and boxing history was forever altered by the Long Count of Round 7.

THE ONE AND ONLY CHAMP

After his first fight with Tunney, in which he had taken a sustained beating to the face, Dempsey had gone home to his movie-star wife with his eyes almost puffed shut. Unwilling to watch her husband endure pain, Estelle Taylor had refused to go to the fight.

Dempsey sat in a darkened room, big dark glasses shielding his bruised, swollen eyes.

"What happened, Ginsberg?" said Estelle, using her pet name for Dempsey.

"I just forgot to duck, honey," replied the battered ex-champ. Dempsey's phrase stuck as a staple of the nation's slang through the rough-and-tumble decade of the thirties, the murderous war years of the forties, and even into the postwar fifties.

Jack Dempsey remained a favorite everywhere in America. For years he could be seen dining at a window table in his eponymous restaurant in Times Square, seated with a beautiful starlet. He was available. He enjoyed the public. He said, "I like being a public figure as much as Joe DiMaggio hates it."

His life came full circle. Once derided as a draft-dodging slacker, Dempsey joined the Coast Guard in World War II. He advanced to the rank of lieutenant commander and at age 49 took part in the invasion of Okinawa.

Most of all, Jack Dempsey remained a tough guy, a heavyweight champ, as Roger Kahn points out anecdotally. "Dempsey was going home one night in the 1960s after dining at his restaurant," Kahn relates. "He lived on 53rd Street. He was wearing his winter attire, a beautifully tailored black cashmere overcoat, and a couple of street punks looked at the elderly gent and decided he was easy pickings for a mugging. As soon as they jumped him, Dempsey went into his crouch and threw some heavy body shots. He dropped them both. They couldn't get up when the cops arrived. Dempsey was 70 years old."

Although I spent 17 years at the side of the greatest fighter in the history of boxing, Muhammad Ali, when I hear someone say *heavyweight champion*, I think of Jack Dempsey first. That's not to say he was better than Ali or, for that matter, my other hero, Joe Louis. It's just a kid's thing, you know; something that goes back to a dish of arroz con pollo one afternoon at the Columbia Restaurant. For me, Jack Dempsey would always would be the one and only Champ.

The great Joe Louis and his longtime trainer, Jack "Chappie" Blackburn, in 1938.
(*Associated Press Photo*)

THE REVENGE

JOE LOUIS vs. MAX SCHMELING
CHAMPION   CHALLENGER

HEAVYWEIGHT CHAMPIONSHIP
JUNE 22, 1938
NEW YORK CITY

ROUND I

In the thirties the world was teetering on the brink of economic uncertainty and ruin. The prevailing socioeconomic systems in Europe and the United States were failing badly, opening the door for radical or dramatic measures ranging from totalitarianism on one side of the Atlantic to the New Deal on the other.

In Russia, Stalin consolidated his stranglehold on the communist state through a series of pogroms, purges, and Five-Year Plans that cost millions of lives. In Italy, Mussolini ruled over a strict fascist state. In Germany, Hitler, the leader of the ascendant National Socialist party, dismantled the Weimar Republic and loosed upon the world a ruthless Nazi regime whose goals were genocide and global conquest. In Spain, a bitter civil war ended with the victory of Francisco Franco and his fascist party.

In America, social order was on the verge of collapse. The Great Depression crippled the nation and gave rise to the election of a powerful leader, Franklin Delano Roosevelt, whose presidential inaugural address bolstered the public's sagging morale with the ringing phrase, "We have nothing to fear but fear itself." The nation withdrew into isolationism, eschewing foreign involvement as it attempted to mend from within.

Americans sought in sports relief from the travails of daily life. It was the era of larger-than-life heroes, and the biggest of these was a black man from Detroit.

Joe Louis, the Brown Bomber, was quiet, shy, and powerful, standing 6 feet 1½ inches tall and possessing a combination of boxing skill and knockout potency never before seen in a heavyweight champion. From the start of his career, in 1934, through early 1938 he had lost only one fight, a 12th-round knockout at the hands of the German Max Schmeling in a June 19, 1936, nontitle bout. A year later, Louis had won the heavyweight crown by knocking out James J. Braddock in the eighth round. Schmeling had captured the vacant heavyweight title by defeating Jack Sharkey in 1930, then lost it in '32 to the same man. The stage thus was set for a Louis-Schmeling rematch. Americans gladly took a respite from their troubles by eagerly anticipating the encounter.

Louis and Schmeling were to meet again in a 15-round heavyweight title bout at Yankee Stadium on June 22, 1938. For Louis the rematch was an opportunity to exact revenge from the man who knocked him out two years earlier, also at Yankee Stadium, in a startling upset.

As it turned out, the rematch would become much more than a diversion from the Depression and Louis's big chance to get even with his lone conqueror. It would become the Fight of the Century to date and an event of international political significance. Adolf Hitler had spread the malignancy of Nazism over much of Europe and was threatening yet another world war. As an emblem of his doctrine of Aryan supremacy, of a master race, Hitler chose an unwitting Max Schmeling, whose duty it would be to go to America, wrest the heavyweight championship of the world from a racial inferior, and bring the championship belt home to Germany.

Newspapers seized upon the fight's racial-political angle, and the American public almost uniformly supported the humble champion, Louis. The irony of Louis's representing the United States during the era of segregation, in which black men were denied the right to vote and endured virtual economic slavery in the South and elsewhere, was not lost on the nation's black leadership. The country's white population regarded Louis (to his amazement) as one of their own. For his part, Louis became one of the first black athletes to weaken the heretofore sturdy walls of racial prejudice, paving the way for Jackie Robinson and others in the following decades to eradicate the color barrier from the American sports scene.

The prefight hype transcended the usual good guy vs. bad guy blather. This became a clash of democracy vs. totalitarianism, the allegedly inferior black race vs. the white "master" race, American vs. Hun. Tickets to the epic showdown sold out instantly.

Emanuel Steward, the highly regarded manager, trainer, cornerman, and guru of Detroit's fabled Kronk Gym, who has helped shape 28 world champions, recalled what he heard about that night in Yankee Stadium:

"Well, having been raised in Detroit, you naturally hear a lot of Joe Louis stories. I don't believe that any athlete in the history of sports was bigger than Joe Louis until Muhammad Ali came along. From what older people have told me about the night when Louis fought Max Schmeling, I feel like I can actually experience what was in the air at the time. It was like 'the day the world stood still.' It was more than a sporting event. It was good against evil. Hitler had created the situation surrounding this rematch, and there was so much drama and emotion in the air that I don't think there will be another event that will equal the tension that was in the world that particular night when they fought. And when you speak to old-timers about whether Ali would have beaten Louis, some of them will tell you that no one could have beaten Joe Louis that night."

Louis was unruffled by the tension and pressure surrounding the upcoming bout. When asked by a newsman if the chilly evening air in Yankee Stadium might bother the fighters, Louis deadpanned, "No, we'll both be wearing gloves."

At age 24, Louis entered the ring as boxing's youngest-ever heavyweight champion. He and Schmeling would perform before 75,000 fans—one of the largest crowds in boxing history—who paid nearly a million dollars at the gate. A ringside seat sold for an unheard-of

Depression-era price of $30, which for many jobholders represented a month's pay.

If Joe Louis was cool and collected entering the bout, the same could not be said for Max Schmeling. Bad news was delivered by his Nazi bosses to Schmeling's dressing room before the fight: his wife, Annie Ondra, a German film actress, had been placed under protective custody by the dreaded SS. Compounding his troubles, a special envoy arrived to deliver an important message from Hitler: "Der Führer commands you to win, as a symbol of Aryan supremacy!"

No wonder that Schmeling appeared dazed during the introduction of the fighters. While many New York sportswriters attributed his demeanor to an abject fear of Joe Louis, it appears that poor Max Schmeling had a lot more on his mind.

All around the nation, few people had anything else but the fight on their mind. Much of America stopped in its tracks the moment the fighters touched gloves in the middle of the ring. Everyone was glued to a radio. The event became a benchmark in the lives of those who were around at the time. To the question "Where were you the night Joe Louis fought Max Schmeling?" every American had a ready answer. No event would so rivet the entire nation until Japanese warplanes appeared in the skies over Hawaii on December 7, 1941.

THE BIG FIGHT

Max Schmeling looked like a man walking to the electric chair as he entered the ring. The crowd booed lustily at the sight of the living symbol, however unwilling, of a dark-hearted, odious nation, Hitler's Germany.

When Joe Louis, the Brown Bomber a.k.a. Alabama Assassin, removed his white robe and stood under the bright ring lights of Yankee Stadium, a thunderous roar of support and affection showered down on the impassive champion. Only his eyes betrayed the fire burning inside him. He was here to defend his title. No ex-champion had ever recaptured his crown, and Louis meant to insure that Schmeling would not be the first. Most of all, Louis had an overriding motivation: revenge for the humiliating 12th-round knockout

Schmeling, a 10–1 underdog, had inflicted on him in this very stadium two years earlier. Schmeling had set the boxing world on its ear: he had stopped the seemingly unbeatable Joe Louis.

Upon viewing the film of the epic rematch, Emanuel Steward offered an analysis of the champion's approach to the bout. "I think that Louis's camp devised a perfect strategy," Steward told me. "Knowing that Schmeling was an intelligent fighter, a thinking fighter, who would analyze and take advantage of your mistakes, Louis trained to fight him close and put pressure on him. Once you get too close to a thinking fighter like Schmeling, he starts to become a nervous wreck because he cannot function when he doesn't have that certain zone of space to operate from. Louis crowded him and punched everything very short—he got right on top of Max before he punched. He didn't throw anything long so that Schmeling could counter. It was just too much for Schmeling to handle."

The Brown Bomber's victory carried symbolic weight on the eve of World War II. (*Wm. C. Greene*)

After brief introductions in the middle of the ring, the fighters were ready to go. Louis needed no last-minute instructions from his corner. He had a game plan: overwhelm and annihilate Schmeling.

Joe started out using his familiar, stalking, one-two-and-jab technique. The jabs fell short at first, but he was just range finding. Meanwhile, Schmeling looked frozen. He seemed content merely to block the famous Louis jab. Perhaps he was waiting for Joe to drop his left after he jabbed, whereupon Max could connect with his powerful right hand and stop Louis again.

The German circled away from the pursuing American, who appeared unhurried but determined. With each jab Louis seemed to be closing the gap between them. From time to time Louis threw a hard right to the body, causing Schmeling to wince. Joe was hurting him—both men knew it—but Schmeling offered no countering shots in response. What was he waiting for?

During the first minute of Round 1, Louis had caught Schmeling with two crisp hooks that snapped his head back. Whenever Joe dropped his right hand, Max got on his horse, attempting to flee the champ's debilitating left jab. In the second minute of the round, Joe blocked the only two punches Max would throw in this match. "This ain't like the last fight," Louis later reported thinking at the time. The round had entered its second minute when Louis pulled the trigger, launching a two-fisted attack that drove Schmeling defensively to the ropes. Louis smelled blood.

Punching with devastating accuracy and force, Louis punished Schmeling with brutal body shots that made Max wince and turn away. His ribs may have been cracked by this time. Schmeling staggered back drunkenly, with Louis in pursuit. The crowd surged to its feet.

Now Louis caught up to his faltering opponent and hammered five shots to his face. Schmeling's eyes went blank; his legs shook. As he started to sink toward the floor, he grabbed the upper strand of rope and held on, like a sheet hung to dry on a clothesline, but he would not hold on for long. Louis did not relent. Schmeling recoiled from an explosive right to his body, howling in pain. Referee Arthur Donovan quickly intervened and gave Schmeling a count of one. Max turned bravely to face his tormentor, and the waiting Louis propelled a perfect right to the jaw. Down went Schmeling for a count of three. Why didn't he take a nine-count, which would have afforded him a respite from his torture? He simply didn't know where he was. He was out on his feet.

"Louis's body punches were unbelievable," says Emanuel Steward. "After Max had been immobilized by a right hand to the kidney, he took a left hook dead in the solar plexus, which paralyzed him. Even though Max was hurt and wanted to fall down, he couldn't even fall."

Adds Steward: "And consider that back then, they were fighting with six-ounce gloves, as compared to the 10-ounce gloves heavyweights use today. So it was virtually a pure fistfight, with Louis's punches so devastating and so short that I don't think any fighter in the world could have gotten away from them."

Louis had moved in close, and everything he threw was short, direct, and damaging. Joe was twisting his body into his punches, and this torque made it difficult for Schmeling to see, let alone time, the incoming shots in order to avoid them. In this vulnerable state Max absorbed five very serious blows to the head.

On the strength of sheer willpower and the instincts of the champion that he had been, Schmeling somehow straightened himself and again faced Louis. Joe resumed pulverizing him with both hands, each punch finding its target. Max went down again, this time rising at the count of two. This was real bravery on display, but the effort was doomed. Louis was now "down" on his punches, in a destructive groove. He hit the defenseless Schmeling with two hooks and a climactic right to the jaw, and the German toppled to the canvas. His trainer, Max Machon, threw in the towel, but referee Donovan kicked it from the ring and counted out Schmeling.

When Louis had beaten James J. Braddock to win the heavyweight title, black America had erupted in wild street celebrations.

When Joe Louis annihilated Aryan superman Max Schmeling to retain that title, all of America hit the streets, in what became a coast-to-coast, all-night celebration.

Joe Louis was America's darling, and to a man, the press corps jumped on the Louis bandwagon.

The great boxing writer Bob Considine condensed what had transpired into this perfect lead: "The battery at Yankee Stadium last night was Joe Louis pitching, Max Schmeling catching."

Schmeling had thrown only two punches while receiving 50 solid blows in a little over two minutes. No round in boxing had so clearly demonstrated the absolute superiority of one boxer over another. No round had meant more to a nation's pride. No previous round had made a black man a hero to all his countrymen and a trailblazer in a movement that would begin to cleanse sports of their racist stain.

Joe Louis earned more than $350,000 for his one-round knockout of Max Schmeling. He won not only the devotion of the American public, but worldwide acclaim for defeating Hitler's handpicked Super-Aryan. "They Can Be Beat," shouted the headlines.

Max Schmeling went directly to a hospital from the scene of the savage beating he had endured. He subsequently joined the German army, as an elite paratrooper. He compiled a distinguished war record, participating by paradrop in the occupation of Crete. He survived his wartime combat and lived out his life honored as a German hero— as the man who once knocked out the immortal Joe Louis.

THE UNTOLD STORY

One of the untold stories about this fight concerns Adolf Hitler's feverish interest in it. So invested in the fight's outcome was Hitler that he ordered top Nazi lieutenant Heinrich Himmler to have his Gestapo pick up and detain Schmeling's mother, father, wife, and children. Hitler's message to Schmeling was clear: "If you choose to defect and stay in America, we will send your family to a concentration camp." Poor Max had plenty to worry about in the spring of 1938: the Brown Bomber on the one hand and the megalomaniacal fuhrer on the other.

Fight night found a worried Schmeling pacing his dressing room before entering the ring. He was far more worried about Himmler's threat than about Joe Louis. After all, he had beaten Joe Louis once before, by a KO, but nobody ever beat Heinrich Himmler and his SS.

The fight was broadcast by transatlantic cable and all of Germany was listening. When it became evident that Louis was dominating Schmeling, someone at the Nazi propaganda ministry pulled the plug. Germans never heard the fight's conclusion.

The next day, a functionary, assuming that the result had been favorable, sent Frau Schmeling a plant and a bouquet of flowers in Hitler's name. I imagine that that functionary ended up taking the place reserved for Schmeling's family at the concentration camp!

While Joe Louis's reputation and confidence both skyrocketed, the man from Lafayette, Alabama, kept his pride in check. He told me about his ego one day in Denver. "Doc," said Louis, "I had as big an ego as Ali, only I chose to keep my mouth shut."

In Joe Louis and Muhammad Ali there existed two gigantic egos, but with good reason. They were the best boxers of their respective times. Each fought for the better part of two decades. They were genuine American heroes. If they didn't have healthy egos, I don't know who would.

Schmeling and his wife, Annie Ondra, appeared cordial in a meeting with Hitler, but Max was an unwilling tool of Nazi propaganda and Ondra a victim of threats by the SS. (*Hank Kaplan Archives*)

Louis KO'd Conn when the Pittsburgh Kid foolishly tried to slug it out with the champ. (*Hank Kaplan Archives*)

JOE LOUIS vs. BILLY CONN
CHAMPION   CHALLENGER

HEAVYWEIGHT CHAMPIONSHIP
JUNE 18, 1941
NEW YORK CITY

ROUND 13

Without question, the forties were the most significant decade of the 20th century. A cataclysmic world war culminated in the downfall of the totalitarian regimes in Germany, Italy, and Japan, but at a cost of over 50 million lives.

From the turmoil of that great conflict arose the imposing figures of Franklin D. Roosevelt, Winston Churchill, Mahatma Gandhi, Charles de Gaulle, and an array of victorious generals: Marshall, Eisenhower, Patton, and MacArthur. To the military lexicon were added new terms: *blitzkrieg*, *U-boat*, and, most portentously, *atomic bomb*.

The decade's two political tragedies were unexpected. FDR, serving an unprecedented fourth term as president, died on April 12, 1945, and so did not live to see the Allied victory he had orchestrated. Perhaps more tragic was the ouster in Britain of Winston Churchill—doubly so, because it occurred at the moment of triumph over the Axis Powers and was provoked by his own constituents.

The second, postwar half of the forties saw a return to normalcy. The Marshall Plan poured billions into rebuilding a shattered

Europe. American soldiers came home; the army was disbanded and returning veterans were offered jobs, housing, and that most precious benefit, the GI Bill of Rights, which provided each serviceman an opportunity to obtain a college education.

At the outset of the forties, as the nation's isolationism began to crack under the inevitability of war, Joe Louis was cruising in his reign as heavyweight champion. Lacking legitimate opponents, the Brown Bomber had settled into a routine of dispatching a "bum of the month." His little-known victims in 1940 included Arturo Godoy (twice), Johnny Paycheck, and Al McCoy. The standard scenario was an early-round knockout. Louis continued business as usual in the early months of '41, disposing of Red Burman (KO, 5) in January and Gus Dorazio

Billy Conn, a rakish Irishman who could box, amassed a career record of 63-12-1. (*International News Photo; Photofest*)

(KO, 2) in February. Abe Simon lasted 13 rounds before he was counted out in March. The following month, Tony Musto hit the canvas for good in Round 9. Buddy Baer, the month of May's bum, was disqualified in the seventh round.

More of the same—that is, a propensity for falling down quickly—was expected from Louis's opponent scheduled for June, a light-heavyweight named Billy Conn. The public and the press ho-hummed the fight; another month, another bum. There was just one problem: Billy Conn wasn't a bum. He was a slick-as-glass boxer, the kind of ring tactician that could cause trouble for the plodding, methodical Louis.

At age 23, Conn was 25 pounds lighter than the well-muscled Louis and looked pale and frail standing next to the champ. Wise guys gave Conn those familiar two chances, slim and none, to win the fight.

"And slim done left town," they added.

THE FIGHT

On the night of June 18, 1941, 54,487 fans paid $450,000 for seats in the Polo Grounds from which they expected to witness Joe Louis's prompt, surgical dissection of the Pennsylvania-born youngster known as the Pittsburgh Kid. It's safe to say that nobody anticipated that Billy Conn would come within 6 minutes and 2 seconds of stealing Joe Louis's heavyweight crown.

It was a warm New York night, three days before summer would officially begin, with the temperature hovering around 80 degrees. Many in the shirtsleeved crowd were looking forward to cashing in on a Louis victory. The champ, who outweighed the challenger 199 to a mere 169, was a 1-to-4 bet to win and 5 to 11 to score a knockout. "Like found money," some fans laughed.

Almost from the opening bell, however, it was evident that the champ was not himself tonight. His movements seemed slow and tentative; he seemed unsure of where to aim his jackhammer left jab. More often than not, Louis hit nothing but air as Conn vanished beyond his reach. For his part Conn was content to flick a harmless jab in Louis's face—an annoyance that repeatedly threw off the champ's timing—and then move away. Round after round, the decisive attack that fans expected from Louis failed to materialize, and gradually the message sunk in: Billy Conn was winning this fight.

Says noted referee Mills Lane, after viewing Conn's display of superior ring generalship in the fight film, "Louis always had problems with movement by his opponents. Joe was not great in dealing with mobility, and that was what Conn utilized to get a big edge. More than halfway through the fight he was way ahead on points."

The fight now entered the final five rounds, which are considered the "championship" rounds—the time when a big fight is won or lost, when men are separated from boys and contenders from pretenders. This was Joe Louis territory. As for his situation on this warm night in the Polo Grounds, Louis was sure that he could knock this kid out, but when would he get the chance?

THE FATEFUL GAMBLE

The rounds came and went—7, 8, 9, 10—and still Louis waited in vain for his opening. Time was running out as Conn was piling up points. Conn knew he was ahead, knew the heavyweight championship of the world was within his grasp. All he had to do was keep boxing, keep sticking and moving. The champion, on the other hand, felt an increasing sense of urgency. He could no longer hope to win a decision. He needed a KO.

Said Louis in his book *My Life: Joe Louis*, "By the time the eighth round came up, I was tired as hell, and I stayed that way until the 12th. The 12th round didn't help. I was completely exhausted, and he was really hurting me with left hooks. I was hoping that he would lose his head and gamble, because I could see myself saying, 'Bye, bye, title!'

"At the end of each round, when I'd hit my corner, me and Chappie [Louis's cornerman Jack Blackburn]would talk. We figured that my strategy would be based on him trying to slug it out with me. He knew I was getting tired and was hoping for a toe-to-toe slugfest. I'd been studying him all night, and I knew if he started to throw a long left hook, I had him.

"At the end of the 12th, Chappie said, 'You're losing on points. You got to knock him out.'"

This Louis knew. Meanwhile, Conn's growing confidence swelled a bit too much. Sometimes overconfidence breeds bad ideas, causing a man to take foolhardy risks—to gamble unwisely. For Billy Conn, this was one of those times. The Pittsburgh Kid decided that capturing the heavyweight crown by a decision over the great Joe Louis wouldn't be enough. He wanted to knock out the great Joe Louis. He came out of his corner for the start of Round 13 planning to do just that.

"In the 13th, Conn got too cocky," said Louis. "He knew, just like I knew, he was winning. But Conn didn't come out boxing now; he made his mistake. He wanted to try and slug it out. We got in a clinch, and he said, 'Joe, you're in for a tough fight tonight.' I just said, 'We'll see.'"

What Louis saw was Conn standing right in front of him, at unbelievably close range. For some reason Conn had abandoned his bewildering evasive tactics and his pesky left jab, which had so frustrated Louis. Now he was laying down the gauntlet, challenging Louis to a slugfest, and Joe was only too happy to oblige. This was Louis's game, and he stepped into the firing zone with a smile.

Louis leaned into several solid body shots. Conn responded with a quick combination, but Louis spotted an opening. Said Louis, "Son of a gun if he didn't start the long left hook I'd been waiting for all night! I zapped a right to his head. He turned numb, and I said to myself, 'I gotcha now!'"

In an instant, the champ was connecting with both hands to Conn's head. A short, chopping right stopped Billy in his tracks, setting him up for a final, lethal flurry that sent him crumbling to the canvas. Referee Eddie Joseph counted him out at 2 minutes and 58 seconds of Round 13. Billy Conn had gambled big, and lost.

For Joe Louis, the fight was an awakening. For once, he found the crowd cheering the underdog and not him, the long-beloved champion He was not used to being booed. It hurt him, and it opened his eyes to the future. He was fallible. He wouldn't always be the people's choice. He could be beaten.

In his subdued postfight dressing room, Billy Conn sat on the rubbing table, a white towel over his head, a cocky smile on his handsome Irish face.

"Why did you do it? Why did you go toe to toe with Joe Louis?" a reporter asked him.

Looking at the newsman with his engaging crooked grin, Billy coolly replied, "What's the use of being Irish if you can't do something stupid once in a while?"

That was Billy Conn, all brash, show-off Irish pub crawler. One of the boys. One of the lads.

His close call with Conn rendered Joe Louis mortal. Other fighters now saw him as beatable. The Brown Bomber fought one more time in 1941, in September against Lou Nova, a strange man who claimed he had a "cosmic punch" that would KO Joe. Louis, a simple man, did not understand the metaphysical implications of the cosmic punch, so he solved things in his usual, straightforward way: he knocked out Lou Nova in six rounds.

Louis immediately volunteered for military service when the nation entered World War II. He turned down an officer's commission. "I want the boys to feel I'm one of them. I want them to slap me on the back and put their arms around my neck. They couldn't do that if I was an officer," he said. During the war he fought hundreds of exhibition rounds in bouts near military facilities, and donated his entire purse from title fights to the war effort.

As he had with Max Schmeling, Louis developed a close friendship with Billy Conn. The men met at a party after the war. Conn joked, "Joe, why didn't you let me hold the title for you during the war? You knew I'd give it back to you."

Joe deadpanned, "Shoot, Billy, I loaned it to you for 13 rounds and you didn't know what to do with it."

They both knew that Billy Conn had thrown away his main chance on that hot night in the Polo Grounds. His foolhardy gamble had blown up in his handsome face.

James P. Dawson, writing in the *New York Times*, called the bout "one of the greatest heavyweight battles of recent years. The struggle was waged in an atmosphere reminiscent of older and better times in boxing. The great crowd saw Conn fight a battle that was true to his style, of necessity, but better than usual, though it proved inadequate. And the crowd saw Louis fight like a champion should, a champion who refuses to become discouraged though he was buffeted about outlandishly at times."

But the veteran sportswriter detected warning signs in Louis's performance. "Unmistakably, Louis has slipped. Even making allowances for style—the contrast in styles is inescapable—the champion is not the Louis of old," Dawson wrote.

"Joe Louis was not sure of himself last night, a fact which might be explained by a circumstance which found him in the ring with a veritable wraith of speed. But the speed that Louis once boasted himself is gone, the accuracy behind his punches is diminishing. He is becoming heavy footed and heavy armed, weaknesses which were reflected as he floundered at times in his quest of the target that was Conn.

"One thing remains undiminished with Joe Louis, and that cannot be denied. He is still an annihilating puncher. His right hand claims a victim whenever it lands. His left hook jars an opponent to his heels, and props him for his finishing potion that is his killer right hand."

JOE LOUIS: AN APPRECIATION

Having seen Joe Louis fight and become friendly with him, I can safely say that he was the most impressive fighter I have witnessed in action, with the exception of Muhammad Ali. They were different fighters and different men, however, so it is not worthwhile to compare them. They were similar in that both had gigantic egos, established and confirmed by their sustained excellence over a long period of time, but Louis was shy and quiet, while Ali, of course, was exhibitionistic, exuberant, fun loving, and outsized in every way.

Louis is the second-best heavyweight I ever saw. I saw Dempsey fight, but as an old man. I saw Marciano in his prime. Neither was as good as Louis.

When you think of Joe Louis, you think of something solid. There was no artifice, no filigree, no shucking, no jiving. What you saw was what you got. He had a good heart and a noble spirit. While Joe Louis was on top, boxing was king.

Says Mills Lane, "I heard Ali, back when he was a fresh, cocky kid named Cassius Clay, ask Joe Louis, 'What if you had to fight me?' And Joe, in that great deadpan way of his, said, 'You know that bum-of-the-month club? You'd be in it.'"

Says the consummate boxing insider, Angelo Dundee, "Joe Louis to me was the finest human being God put on this earth in every way. I met him in 1944, and we were buddies till he died. Let me tell you, I'm a guy that saw Rocky Marciano knock him out, and I cried because I felt so bad for Joe Louis. He was—how can I say it?—he was Wheaties, he was Campbell's Soup, he was everything American. He was Joe Louis."

And how would Dundee instruct one of his fighters to deal with Louis?

"I wouldn't stay directly in front of Joe Louis," says the renowned

After defeating Conn in '41, Louis fought twice the following year, donating all of his earnings from those bouts to the war effort. (*Photofest*)

trainer. "I would give him angles to cope with, and a stiff, fast jab. Once Louis got you on the end of a punch you were gone, because he would hit you with four or five punches. He was a very strong puncher with either hand, and his jab was poetic. Joe Louis was a complete heavyweight champ of the world."

In my mind, the Joe Louis of boxing writers was little Jimmy Cannon. He was a bitter, ruthless man, but a jewel of a writer on the sweet science. His evaluations of boxers were flawless, and he would call it exactly as he saw it, even if that meant knocking a friend. He and Louis were great friends. Cannon venerated Louis, but could take him to task in print if necessary.

It seems fitting, then, to conclude with Cannon's appraisal of Louis—a great writer on a great boxer.

"There was conceit in Joe Louis, but he controlled it," Cannon wrote. "There was a lot of pride in him too, but it never took charge of him. He was shy, but he hid it in silence when there were strangers around. He was easy-going and good company if you were a friend. I admired him, but I tried to see him clearly. At the end, when he needed sympathy but I knew he was a goner and said so, he never complained about it, and it never spoiled our relationship.

"He was a great champion, and I'm glad he was a champion in my time. He was mean at his work, but he was able to leave it in the ring. The cruelty was there all right. The poverty of his childhood formed him as it does all fighters. He was never resentful, and he always did the best he could. His best was wonderful.

"The night Marciano knocked him out, a guy said it was pretty sad to see a great champ get knocked out.

"'I've knocked out lotsa guys,' said Louis.

"He was a fighter. Many guys make a good living fighting for money, and some become champions. They can show you licenses to prove they are fighters, and there isn't any way I can dispute them. But Louis was a boy's dream of a fighter. There was joy and innocence in his skills, and this gave him what the others lacked. There have been others, but I am sure of Joe Louis.

"Joe Louis was a fighter. It is the finest compliment I can give him."

Boxing legend Sugar Ray Robinson, five-time winner of the world middleweight crown. (*Photofest*)

THE ST. VALENTINE'S DAY MASSACRE

SUGAR RAY ROBINSON
CHALLENGER

VS.

JAKE LaMOTTA
CHAMPION

MIDDLEWEIGHT CHAMPIONSHIP

FEBRUARY 14, 1951
CHICAGO

ROUND 13

The 1950s was a golden age for boxing, thanks to the advent of television. No sport was more telegenic. A boxing match had only two contestants, transpired under bright lights that produced a good picture, and could be televised from any arena, anywhere. Beer and razor-blade companies created and sponsored hugely popular weekly fights on TV. The public chose its favorite fighters and followed them closely on the "small screen."

The fifties yielded a bountiful crop of popular champions, including Kid Gavilan, with his "bolo" punch; Gene Fullmer, "the Mormon Middleweight"; Paddy de Marco; Ike Williams; Willie "Will o' the Wisp" Pep; Dick Tiger of Nigeria; Beau Jack; Ralph Dupas; Archie Moore, the Old Mongoose; and Joey Maxim.

The most popular televised boxing show was *Friday Night Fights*, sponsored by Gillette. The commentator was Dan Dunphy, whose crisp, sparse style and penchant for accuracy made him the most credible of the day's blow-by-blow announcers and commentators.

Boxing's biggest attraction at the outset of the fifties was unquestionably Joe Louis, but the Bomber was nearing the end of his long, storied career, having come out of a one-year retirement in 1950 only to lose a 15-round decision to Ezzard Charles for the heavyweight title. The end came on October 26, 1951, when Rocky Marciano, a young, tough caveman of a fighter from Brockton, Massachusetts, knocked Louis out in the eighth round in New York. The nation watched on TV as Joe Louis fought for the last time.

The heir to Joe Louis was his best friend, Sugar Ray Robinson, who was nearly too good a boxer to be believed. In appearance and style he was diametrically opposed to Louis. Sugar Ray was a sleek, slick, handsome man, with amazing reflexes and quicksilver leg speed—a sports car to Louis's Mack truck. Louis had been hailed as a hero for his wartime military service. Robinson had been arrested as a deserter. In the ring, Louis exhibited a deliberate, plodding style and heavy, explosive punches. Robinson was a dance master, capable of raining a storm of pinpoint punches from a bewildering array of angles.

If there was ever a fighter who was made for television, it was Sugar Ray Robinson. He was thrilling to watch, not only on account of his masterly boxing skills, but also because of his great courage. Among his memorable bouts in the fifties were battles (including, in many cases, stirring rematches) with Carl "Bobo" Olson, Randy Turpin, Rocky Graziano, Joey Maxim, Paul Pender, and Carmen Basilio.

Perhaps Robinson's most memorable fight in the fifties took place on February 14, 1951—St. Valentine's Day— in Chicago, when the Detroit-born Sugar Ray, at age 29 the reigning world welterweight champion, sought to wrest the middleweight title from the Bronx Bull, Jake LaMotta, also 29. The two fighters knew each other well, having previously met five times, with Robinson winning four of those bouts. When Robinson and LaMotta signed for a sixth match, American boxing fans looked forward to what promised to be a bloody, hard-fought bout.

MEETING MR. GREY

By 1951, Sugar Ray Robinson had established himself as the finest welterweight ever to hold the crown. His combination of boxing wizardry and devastating punching power had earned him a reputation as the world's best fighter of any weight class. Having dispensed with all competition in the welterweight division and grown tired of struggling to stay within the division's weight limit, he decided to move up a class and vie for the middleweight title.

The immediate problem was that the title was held by one of the toughest men in the fistic world, Jake LaMotta. LaMotta, a rugged, hard-hitting puncher, had a couple of other distinguishing characteristics: close ties to the mob and a consuming hatred of Sugar Ray Robinson.

In his book *Sugar Ray*, written with Dave Anderson, Robinson recounts an ominous incident. He is instructed to meet a "Mr. Grey" at an isolated location. Mr. Grey was the name Frankie Carbo used

A done deal: LaMotta and Robinson formalize plans for their Chicago middleweight title bout as Joe Triner, chairman of the Illinois State Athletic Commission, looks on. (*Associated Press Photo*)

in his boxing dealings. Carbo was a top mobster, whom no one defied and managed to live long thereafter.

In their shadowy meeting, Mr. Grey made Sugar Ray an offer he didn't think the boxer could refuse. "I want you to have three fights with LaMotta," Robinson said Mr. Grey told him. "The first, you win. The next, Jake wins. The third is on the up and up."

"You got the wrong guy," said Robinson nervously.

"Three fights is a lot of money," said Mr. Grey.

"Tell LaMotta to keep his hands up and his ass off the floor. Tell him to be sure to do that when the bell rings," said Sugar Ray.

Robinson now felt some pressure. It wasn't easy to say no to a man like Frankie Carbo, who not only had a knack for influencing boxing judges and referees, but was known to be capable of inflicting bodily harm. Sugar believed that to win the fight, he'd have to knock out LaMotta.

Whether this story is absolutely true is a moot point. What is known is that Mr. Grey ran afoul of the law and entered the federal penitentiary in Atlanta in 1961.

I watched the film of the St. Valentine's Day Massacre with the ebullient cornerman Lou Duva, who has been a fixture in boxing for half a century and is a member of the sport's Hall of Fame. He has managed hundreds of fighters and helped develop many champions. He has been a close friend of Jake LaMotta, among others, so it was natural to seek Lou's take on the reported meeting between Sugar Ray and Mr. Grey.

Lou smiled his sly smile. "In the fifties you could choreograph almost any fight you wanted to—if the right people were there making the calls." A fight's outcome could be fixed even when the bout took place under the scrutinizing lens of a TV camera, added Lou.

Robinson crossed paths with Carbo one more time, in 1966, following an exhibition bout at the prison where the mobster resided. The men shook hands, and Mr. Grey left the boxer with these parting words: "Say hello to the Bull for me."

THE FIGHT

Looking back on what came to be called the St. Valentine's Day Massacre, Jake LaMotta said, later in his life, "To this day, I don't know whether it was Robinson or the weight that licked me. When you are young you can reduce yourself to a shadow and keep your strength, but as you get older, you can't. The first time we fought, in 1942, I made the 160-pound limit easy. Three weeks later, I weighed 182. Now it was nine years later. I was faced with the same problem multiplied by nine. I started training weighing 187. I was a light heavyweight fighting for the middleweight title."

LaMotta tried to make the weight limit for his sixth clash with Robinson by using a classic technique—starving himself—yet he was still four pounds too heavy the night before the fight. His trainers pushed him into a steam bath and dosed him with laxatives and diuretics. At 10 in the morning of the weigh-in the next day, he tipped the scales at 160 on the nose.

Sugar Ray Robinson was the master of the psyche-out. On this occasion he decided to confront LaMotta with a bit of bizarre behavior. As they sat next to each other at a press luncheon before the fight, Robinson summoned the waiter.

"Would you ask the chef if I could have a glass of beef blood?" he inquired.

The waiter looked at Jake, who shrugged.

"Don't you know that the great Joe Louis drinks eight ounces of blood every day for three weeks before a fight?" Robinson asked his opponent.

"Oh," said LaMotta, looking sick to his stomach, "what does that do for you?"

"It gives you strength for the last kick, rounds 10 to 15. Don't you see how strong Joe Louis is in the last rounds?" replied Ray.

Jake considered this information, then shook his head decisively. "Man, I don't need that. I'm not drinking no blood."

Sugar Ray smiled. He knew he had hooked his sucker; now he reeled him in. "Yeah, Jake, that's why I'm going to be beating your ass from 10 to 15. I'll be strong. You'll be weak."

LaMotta shuddered again at the thought of swallowing blood. "Yeah, well, that is just a lot of shit. I ain't drinking blood!"

LaMotta left the press luncheon highly agitated and remained so for the rest of the day. Later, working out at the gym, he asked around: Is it true? Are there fighters who drink blood to gain strength?

"Don't you?" replied the old boxing retainers, driving LaMotta deeper into confusion and despair.

"I ain't drinking no blood," repeated Jake. Seeking comfort from his beautiful blonde wife, Vicky, and his brother Joey, he found none. "Why not?" they both asked.

Robinson had artfully psyched out LaMotta. Not long before fight time, however, Jake had an epiphany. Passing a liquor store, he divined the solution to his dilemma. He would buy a fifth of cognac, wrap the bottle in white tape to resemble a water bottle, and carry the disguised container into the ring. Thus fortified, he could not be knocked out. He might lose a

Sugar Ray brutally battered the Bronx Bull for most of 13 rounds, winning on a TKO. (*Hank Kaplan Archives*)

decision, but he wouldn't give Robinson the satisfaction of a knockout. Sugar Ray Robinson has his blood, Jake LaMotta has his cognac.

In describing this incident in his book *Raging Bull: My Story*, LaMotta explains, "The cognac wasn't to give me strength; it was to give me false courage, and what is false courage really but true fear. What the brandy was doing was helping me avoid the fact that I was absolutely in no shape to go against an opponent as good as Sugar Ray."

Film footage of the fight's brutal closing rounds shows a battered LaMotta doggedly refusing to go down. He is being pounded, while his face grows increasingly unrecognizable; a grotesque, bloody mess. Sportswriters at ringside were appalled. One of them, Al Buck, wrote in the *New York Post*, " . . . the bleeding, bruised and battered Bronx Bull was still on his feet, but nobody would want to see that slaughter again."

Could this badly hurt but still upright fighter have been drunk?

Says Lou Duva, "You know, it's tough to knock down a drunk. Yeah, LaMotta could have drunk himself out of the fight. It's a good thing they stopped it. He could have been killed. Sugar Ray's punches and combinations, and the way Ray was so fresh out there . . . he could have done whatever he wanted to LaMotta. Looking at this fight, you know that they gave Robinson the right label: 'pound for pound, the greatest fighter that ever lived.' I believe that."

THE TOUGH 13TH

Here is how LaMotta recalled those last rounds, when he refused to go down despite suffering a fearsome beating: "I was ahead by the 10th round, but I knew I didn't have gas for the last five. I kept thinking, 'All right, you son of a bitch, you are not going to put me down. Nobody's ever decked Jake LaMotta, and (the first one) is not going to be you. If that is as hard as you can hit, you must have been fighting pushovers all this time. Let's see how hard you can hit, you son of a bitch.'"

To this day, many old-timers maintain that this was the fiercest whipping they ever saw one champion inflict on another. In the 13th round the only thing holding LaMotta up was the top rope, to which he clung by one arm.

LaMotta had nothing left on his punches, and his balance was failing fast. Still, he shuffled toward Robinson, who waited for him like a man with a loaded gun.

"You can't do it, you black bastard," LaMotta growled. "You can't put me on the deck." Blood flowed from his nose as Robinson peppered his face with hammering jabs. Jake's eyes were nearly closed, but still the Bronx Bull lurched forward. Robinson retreated, set, and fired off a six-punch combination that staggered LaMotta to a standstill. Robinson now began a classical attack, pounding the body and head as LaMotta reeled from rope to rope. The beating continued in a corner, but LaMotta somehow stayed on his feet. Robinson looked quizzically at referee Frank Sikora. At first the ref made no move to intervene. In a championship match of this magnitude, he would give the defending champion every chance to turn the tide. But yet more blows from Robinson fell on the helpless LaMotta as Round 13 wound down, and Sikora acted at last, waving Robinson away from his bleeding quarry. This savage fight was over.

Sugar Ray Robinson was the new middleweight champion of the world, but Jake LaMotta had preserved what was for him a point of honor. "You didn't put me on the deck, Robinson," said LaMotta when the fighters met in the middle of the ring. "You got my title, but you didn't put me on the deck."

Robinson admired LaMotta's toughness—how the Bull always stood in his corner between rounds, his leopard-skin robe thrown over his shoulders, refusing to sit down. Jake had been his usual self at the end of the fight, ignoring the concerned cornermen huddled around him and snarling disgustedly at the doctor who tried to examine him. These men proffered their hands to help him down the ring stairs; LaMotta slapped them away.

But after reaching his dressing room, finally, Jake LaMotta collapsed. Oxygen was needed to revive him, and it took the Bronx Bull two hours to recover enough strength to leave the arena.

AFTER THE FIGHT

Sugar Ray Robinson had won the middleweight title and in doing so had beaten Jake LaMotta five out of six times. On this occasion Robinson had been thoroughly dominant, but LaMotta's courage had captured the crowd's admiration. Somehow, the Bull had managed to avoid the first knockdown of his career.

Both men lived full lives after the fight. In 1952 Robinson successfully defended his middleweight title twice, winning a March decision over Bobo Olson and knocking out Rocky Graziano a month later in the third round. He solidified his reputation as history's best "pound for pound" boxer and continued fighting until his retirement in 1965. As we'll see shortly, however, he stayed around too long. On April 12, 1989, three weeks before his 68th birthday, he died of Alzheimer's disease. He was inducted posthumously into the International Boxing Hall of Fame in 1990.

Jake led a wild postfight life that included many wives and children, arrests, and jail time. He fought until 1954 and subsequently worked as a standup comic. His turbulent life was chronicled in the movie *Raging Bull*, which was based on his book and starred Robert De Niro.

Looking back on the landmark fight, Sugar Ray pointed out that he went into it in the best shape of his life. He credited his extraordinary stamina during the bout to his habit of drinking fresh beef blood.

After the fight, LaMotta had this to say: "Robinson never hurt me. I almost knocked him out in the 11th, but he got away." Sugar Ray's assessment was gracious. "LaMotta didn't lose," he said. "Something had to happen to keep him from winning. Jake LaMotta was a gladiator, too, when he wanted to be."

The blistering 13th round marked the end of one of the most brutal rivalries in boxing history. Sugar Ray Robinson's place in boxing annals was secured by that epic round, while Jake LaMotta's name would become synonymous with (apart from less flattering qualities) dogged, tenacious courage in the ring.

THE END OF THE TRAIL

Some champions get lucky: after being knocked out by a young, up-and-coming contender, they decide to retire. They never fight again, instead embarking on the path to a more tranquil existence.

But these men are a distinct minority. Most veteran boxers continue to fight on well past their prime. In the end they're reduced to losing to nonentities, while collecting tiny paychecks and jeopardizing their health.

The public, refusing to believe that a once-great fighter's skills have vanished and their longtime hero is no longer an even adequate competitor, continues to support the old derelict, turning out for his fights and hoping for the best.

My sole experience with this phenomenon was singularly impressive. Aside from Joe Louis, my boxing hero was Sugar Ray Robinson. By the sixties he was a shadow of himself. He looked just like the old, fabled Sugar Ray, but he fought like someone else, like a mere mortal. When Robinson arrived in Miami Beach in 1963 to fight Ralph Dupas in a bout promoted by Chris Dundee, his once-lordly entourage was reduced to a single trainer.

At that time I was working on a voluntary basis as the doctor for all boxers affiliated with the 5th Street Gym. I was delighted to be asked to treat Sugar Ray, who was taking a variety of medications and nutrients. He demanded hands-on medical care. He liked to be babied.

Sugar Ray was very personable, a delightful storehouse of boxing tales. He was also still a great ladies' man, who held court every night at the Sir John nightclub in the Overtown district. As always, women lined up seeking his favors.

I was asked to work in Robinson's corner during the fight, which didn't figure to last long. I was thrilled by the invitation to assist one of boxing's genuine gods. He still looked sensational, but I would have to see him in action before I could evaluate what remained of his boxing skills.

It was almost immediately apparent that in the ring was a boxer who appeared identical to Sugar Ray Robinson but was an impostor. I looked at Sugar Ray's trainer, who just shrugged. A feeling of sadness and despair crept over me. Robinson won that fight, although the outcome didn't really matter. Despite declining skills, he kept fighting; in 1965, the year in which he reached age 44, Ray fought 15 times—sometimes winning, sometimes losing, but always deteriorating—before finally announcing his retirement on December 10. Even as expansive an ego as Sugar Ray's couldn't recognize the cruel joke he was playing on himself and his public.

In the months preceding his retirement, Sugar Ray Robinson had exemplified the over-the-hill fighter whose skills are shot but who can't bring himself to quit. The same syndrome has affected many other formerly great champions, including, unfortunately, Muhammad Ali.

Said Ali after his exit from the sport, "I could see the shot coming, but I couldn't block it fast enough. I could see an opening for a punch, but by the time my brain sent the message to my hand to move, the opportunity was no longer there."

Exactly. Punching and defense are the products of reflexes and skills. Boxing is not a thinking game; it's a reflex game, and one of the signature features of aging is loss of elasticity and reflex capacity.

So I learned early in my involvement in boxing to watch for the signs that a fighter is slipping, when he will suddenly discover that "It ain't your night, kid." It is very difficult to convince a boxer that his skills have irreversibly eroded and it's time to quit. I believe that boxers no longer belong in the ring after the age of 35. Yes, I am aware that there have been a few exceptions. I also know that history's Archie Moores and George Foremans are few and far between.

Rocky Marciano and trainer Charley Goldman shared a pensive moment between work-outs for the upcoming meeting with heavyweight champion Jersey Joe Walcott. (*Associated Press Photo*)

ROCKY MARCIANO
VS.
JERSEY JOE WALCOTT

CHALLENGER   **CHAMPION**

HEAVYWEIGHT CHAMPIONSHIP

SEPTEMBER 23, 1952
PHILADELPHIA

ROUND 13

For many boxing fans in the early 1950s, television remained a wondrous new medium that magically brought big fights right into their living room. In a few pockets of the country, color TV was introduced, to the amazement of those who sampled it.

Television's major contribution to boxing was the creation of champions who became familiar throughout the country. Now, a bout between big-name boxers traveled well beyond a live crowd in a New York arena, to reach the four corners of America. Fighters such as Sugar Ray Robinson became household names, and their televised exploits were eagerly consumed.

No wonder, then, that a huge national audience awaited the September 23, 1952, heavyweight championship showdown in Philadelphia between Rocky Marciano and Jersey Joe Walcott.

When Joe Louis's intense light began to dim at the end of the forties, boxing aficionados predicted a long fallow period for the heavyweight division. There was nobody in sight to take the place of the great Louis and his 25 title defenses. Boxing would eventually die, some said, because the conventional wisdom was that as the heavyweights go, so goes boxing.

Louis had petered out in a series of unsatisfying fights with an ex-longshoreman, Jersey Joe Walcott, and a light heavyweight, Ezzard Charles, who puffed up to make the heavyweight ranks. For the young Joe Louis, both fighters would have qualified for bum-of-the-month status. But now an old, tired Joe Louis had to struggle to beat both men. Instead of dispatching them via first-round KOs, as he would have in his prime, Louis had to depend on charitable decisions by judges who couldn't bear to see the grand old champion lose his crown on anything but a decisive knockout.

Meanwhile, in Brockton, Massachusetts, a young boxer was growing into a credible contender. He wasn't tall, but he was broad. He couldn't box a lick, but he could knock down a building with a punch, and he seemed immune to pain; the kid could take a punch as well as give one. The gag line was, "If you miss Rocky with a punch, he apologizes to you."

Rocky Marciano, born Rocco Francis Marchegiano on September 1, 1923, was a determined young man on a mission. He loved his gentle Italian immigrant father, Pierino. The elder Marchegiano was exhausted from a lifetime of work at the machines of a shoe factory. He looked and felt older than his 56 years. In 1951, Rocky had earned a match against a "name" opponent, Rex Layne, who was a tough heavyweight contender. He would enjoy a decent payday from the fight, so Rocky informed his father that his days at the shoe factory were over; he was retired. Rocky had by now assumed the duties of the head of his family, and his sense of responsibility fueled his quest for the title. On July 12, 1951, in New York, Rocky KO'd Layne in the sixth round.

Sportswriters began to take notice of the Brockton Blockbuster, but their reviews weren't entirely favorable. "Punches hard, takes a good shot, but is slow, awkward, out of balance, and pathetically amateurish," went one dismissive notice. Such slights only made Rocky, a zealot for training, work harder.

Marciano fought seven times in 1951, knocking out six of his opponents—none of the victims lasted more than nine rounds—and winning the other bout by unanimous decision. The last of the six men he knocked out, and the only one whose name signified much, was Joe Louis, in his final fight. On October 26, on a sad night for the nation, Rocky Marciano, with tears in his eyes, knocked out the old, slow Brown Bomber. Boxing fans mourned the end of a great champion, but acknowledged at the same time that a star had been born.

In 1952 boxing underwent one of its periodic investigations. A very rich, cultured Chicagoan with a taste for vulgarity and an attraction to the messy world of boxing promotion was at the center of events. Along with some shady figures, he formed the International Boxing Commission and promptly monopolized the sport. The man's name was Jim Norris.

An ensuing investigation put the shady gang in jail, broke up the IBC, and helped put Rocky Marciano in line for a heavyweight title fight. First, however, Marciano's manager, who was also matchmaker for the IBC, obliged Rocky to fight Harry "Kid" Matthews. If Marciano won, he would fight Jersey Joe Walcott for the heavyweight crown. On July 28, 1952, in New York, the Rock demolished Matthews in two rounds of seldom-before-seen ring mayhem. He had fulfilled his end of the bargain, earning that title shot against Walcott.

The reigning heavyweight champion of the world was the direct opposite of Rocky Marciano. Jersey Joe Walcott (whose given name was Arnold Raymond Cream) had turned pro at age 16 in 1930, when Rocky was just seven years old. It had taken Jersey Joe 21 years to win the title. He had been a run-of-the-mill fighter, with a record of 53 wins, an eye-catching 16 losses, and one draw. Compared to Marciano's stunning record—entering the Walcott bout, he had won all 42 of his fights, 37 by KO—Jersey Joe's résumé was mediocre.

But Jersey Joe had had a strange career. He got better as he got older. Between bouts he worked as a longshoreman on the tough

Jersey docks. By the time Joe Louis's career was winding down, Walcott's was revving up. He was a crafty boxer, with an unusual style that confused opponents. He would seem to be walking away, then would unleash a powerful left hook. He could counterpunch with the best of them and packed plenty of power. This would not be an easy fight for Rocky.

Walcott had gained the nation's attention as the challenger in two fights for Joe Louis's heavyweight crown. Jersey Joe beat Louis in the first match, in 1947, except the Louis-loyal judges didn't see it that way and awarded the champ the decision. In a return bout the following year, Jersey Joe was repeating his earlier performance when Louis dug deep into his reserves of greatness and managed an 11th-round KO of Walcott.

Jersey Joe continued to fight all the top contenders until he worked his way into a 1949 bout against Ezzard Charles for the title Louis had vacated with his retirement. Charles won both that encounter and a March 7, 1951, rematch by decisions, but Jersey Joe got his revenge on July 18, 1951, with a seventh-round knockout of Charles that gave him the title he had sought for so long. Walcott retained the crown with a decision over Charles on June 5, 1952.

And now the stage was set for Rocky Marciano vs. Jersey Joe Walcott, in what would be the first of two battles.

THE FIGHTERS

Rocky Marciano took his small staff and some family members to the Catskill Mountains in upstate New York to prepare for the fight. He had accustomed himself to a brutally rigorous training regime, in which he lived like a hermit and pushed himself to the limit. He knew what was riding on the fight. His entire family was dependent on him. He felt beholden, too, to the Italian population of Massachusetts that faithfully supported him.

During his training, Marciano had put in 85 rounds of boxing to Jersey Joe's 30. One of Rocky's sparring partners had also worked for Joe Louis. Asked to compare the fighters' respective punching power, he said, "Louis is harder with a barrage of punches, but Rocky hurts you more with one punch than Louis does with four. Rocky hurts every time he hits you."

Lou Duva, a close friend of Marciano's, offers this evaluation of Rocky's style: "You had to beat him, from when the first bell rings to the 15th bell. You could never get him out of there, maybe because he was always pressing you, hitting you, tapping you; hitting you on the shoulder, hitting you on your arm, hitting you in your ribs. He was always doing something. He was going low, coming out of the crouch. He would bob and weave. He had his own style of bobbing and weaving. Charley Goldman, his great trainer, taught him that. But he put so much pressure on you, you had to fight or run out of that ring."

Rocky had a manager whom he genuinely detested. Al Weill was a tough, nickel-and-dime cheapskate who treated Rocky like a prized cow. Weill was genuinely paranoid, too, imagining plots and danger where none existed. One thing he did have was Rocky's name on a tough-to-break contract.

An unusual complication arose before the fight. The bout was a natural for New York. A big gate was predicted, but Jersey Joe's manager, Felix Bocchicchio, had a criminal record and would be legally barred from a fight held in New York. Thus thwarted, Felix insisted on moving the fight to Philadelphia. Since Walcott was from Camden, New Jersey, just outside Philly, the match would take place in the champ's backyard. Bocchicchio, drawing on his gangster background, had the contract amended to guarantee a return match if Walcott lost. Moreover, each side's percentage of the gate would be the same for both fights.

Marciano was so single-mindedly dedicated to his training that he paid no mind to the contractual arrangements. But as the fight approached and Weill's paranoia and possessiveness escalated, Rocky began to get angry. He had a passive nature when it came to everything except his family, especially his father, who was now a full-time presence in his Catskills training camp. One night, Rocky's father got hungry and went to the camp kitchen for a snack. The chef, Alfred Reinauk, who was on loan from

Grossinger's resort, had been ordered by Weill not to open the kitchen at night. Reinauk unceremoniously evicted the elder Marciano from the premises. An irate Rocky gave Weill a thorough chewing out, but the sensitive family matters didn't end there.

Weill hated to see Rocky's wife, Barbara, visit the camp. He did everything to discourage her appearances. "Fighter's wives hurt fighters," he would say, parroting ancient gym lore. In those days boxing managers and trainers looked on sex as the ruination of a fighter. Another hoary motto went like this: "A good lay ruins the fighter for a bout. A good blow job ruins him forever." A book on the training of fighters, by crusty Nat Fleischer, the longtime editor and publisher of *The Ring* magazine, included this chapter title: "Masturbation Is the Scourge of Western Civilization."

Weill's superstitions and demons loomed so large that he forbade Marciano from talking to his wife on the phone during the last two weeks before the fight. Other forms of communication between them, even letters, were also forbidden, and Rocky was not allowed to shake hands or ride in a car in the week leading up to the bout. Weill permitted Marciano to give short interviews to reporters, but reading any news coverage of his upcoming fight was ruled off-limits.

Weill's obsessions and possessiveness drove Marciano crazy. In the past, the manager's involvement with the IBC and its troubles had kept him from spending much time around his fighter. Now he was always around, to Rocky's dismay. Marciano had a disconcerting thought as the day of the fight drew near: Al Weill might want to work his corner. Indeed, Weill insisted on being the third cornerman on the team.

"I want only Allie Colombo and Charley Goldman in the corner," Rocky said firmly. "I seem to do better when they are there." Weill hit the roof. "Absolutely not!" he replied. "You think I would bring you all this way and then not be in the corner for the big one?

"OK," Rocky relented, seeking to avoid trouble this close to the fight. "I just thought you should know how I feel." It was the first crack in a dam of resentment that, now open wide, would unleash each man's hatred of the other and lead to a parting of their ways.

Things got so strange before the fight that Colombo asked Steve Melchiore, a Philadelphia police detective, to accompany him to the boxing commission's office to pick up some fight tickets. Inside the commission office they found Blinky Palermo, a known underworld power in boxing; Felix Bocchicchio, Jersey Joe's manager; and Charles Daggert, who was to be the referee for the fight. Alarm bells went off in Melchiore's head, and he went off to investigate.

Meanwhile, most of Italian Massachusetts was in Philly, trying to place bets on the Brockton Blockbuster. Many had wagered their houses and cars, while others had taken out loans—all fervent expressions of faith in their favorite son, Rocky Marciano.

"I wasn't going to let anybody down. There was too much at stake," Rocky said years later, when informed of the enormous amount his friends and neighbors had bet on his success against Jersey Joe Walcott.

THE FIGHT

The September 23, 1952, fight unfolded before 40,379 fans, who paid $504,645 to see the heavyweight battle. The odds were generally even, perhaps slightly favoring Walcott.

In the hour before he would enter the ring, Marciano lay on the training table in his dressing room, a towel over his eyes. Nearby, little Charley Goldman babbled prefight instructions.

"You gotta bully him, Rock. You gotta take over right away. Show who's boss. Don't let this guy think he can handle you, don't make him brave. But be careful. Don't get careless. Walcott can bang."

Over and over, Goldman repeated his mantra, while Marciano dozed peacefully on the training table. "He hears me," said Charley to no one in particular. What Rocky didn't hear was someone's voice awakening him 30 minutes before the opening bell, as expected, to insure that he'd enter the ring on time. Suddenly, there was an urgent call for him to rush to his corner, with only minutes to go before the bell. There would be no time to warm up. Had there been an innocent breakdown in communication, or was someone trying to sabotage Marciano's title shot?

In the ring Colombo was raging. Rocky shrugged off his late entrance. "I'll warm up in the first round," he said. Meanwhile, standing at ringside was Detective Melchiore, wearing a worried look. Grabbing Marciano's arm as the fighter climbed the stairs to his corner, Melchiore delivered some troubling news. He had found out some things that worried him.

"Listen to me, Rock," said the detective. "You gotta knock him out to win. They got the ref."

The Rock went down in Round 1, but he was up before the ref's count reached three. (*United Press Photo*)

Rocky heard him, but barely; he was in another zone, enveloped by the roar of the surrounding crowd. There is nothing like the electricity of a fight crowd before the opening bell. At midring for the introductions, neither fighter would look at the other. Both yearned for the bell to sound.

At last it did. The crowd howled like a wounded beast. The time for licensed violence had arrived.

Marciano shot from his corner, ready to go—no feeling-out, no jabbing, no starting slowly in order to size up his foe. Walcott came out fast, too, full of steam and thunder. After landing an undamaging combination, Jersey Joe suddenly connected with a zinging left hook, and to the astonishment of everyone, down went Rocky. The crowd gasped with a single, massive intake of air, then roared, smelling blood.

There was Marciano, on the seat of his trunks, looking at his corner in embarrassment, unhurt but surprised.

"Take an eight!" yelled Charley Goldman.

But Rocky had never been down before in his life. Instinctively, before the count reached three, he got up, wiping his gloves on his trunks. His eyes were clear. He felt good.

Walcott, eyes agleam at the prospect of an early knockout, waded in, punching hard, landing some bombs but missing with other shots. Marciano was not standing still. He was winging solid shots of his own to the 38-year-old champ's body.

Walcott winced as the challenger's punches thudded into his midsection, but responded with short, hard blows that found their mark. The end of the fierce first round found Rocky walking to his corner with the taste of blood in his mouth and a swelling sensation in his left eye. With only one round fought, he could barely see.

Throughout the first half of the fight, Marciano fought the only way he knew how: straight ahead, taking three shots if necessary to land one. Walcott was nearly two inches taller and 12 pounds heavier, with a seven-inch reach advantage and many more years of hardscrabble experience in a tough line of work. This was his title, which he had waited so long to obtain. He wasn't about to surrender it to some youngster who fought as if he were cornered in an alley.

In the sixth round Marciano charged in his bull-like crouch and butted heads with Jersey Joe. When they were pulled apart, blood flowed down Rocky's face. A cut—straight, deep, and worrisome—had opened at his hairline. Across the ring, Jersey Joe returned to his corner bearing a deep gash near his left eye. Red splotches began to cover the ring apron and the referee's shirt.

Charley Goldman worked on his man's cut. In those days you could apply anything that would stop the bleeding. The substance used in most championship fights was called Dynamite, and for good reason: it was dangerous.

This corrosive substance actually was ferric chloride, also known as Monzell's Solution. It burned the tissues, thereby coagulating the blood vessels. The danger lay in its getting into the eye, where it would blind a boxer. In the old days, before boxers were attended by real ring physicians, the Dynamite was not surgically removed before cuts were stitched, leaving thick scars that were liable to pop open.

On this night Colombo had apparently made the mistake of continuing to squeeze a sponge filled with water over Marciano's head. With the Dynamite still fresh in the wound, rivulets of water conducted the dangerous substance into Rocky's eyes. The fighter yelped in pain.

"I can't see! My eyes are burning!" he screamed.

"Ya gotta fight, Rock," said Goldman, pushing Rocky back into the ring after trying to wipe his eyes clean with a towel.

Had Walcott been aware of his opponent's blindness, he might have kept a safe distance between them and contented himself with dismantling Marciano with an endless series of pop shots. Instead, the men went toe to toe, and amid the intense action, Jersey Joe failed to notice a change in Rocky.

At the end of Round 7, Rocky's eyes were in even worse shape. Freddie Brown, hired by Al Weill as a cut man and an additional, "insurance" presence in the corner, went to work on Marciano, wiping his eyes with clean sponges soaked with cold water. Slowly, the eyes began to clear up.

At ringside, Weill was going bonkers, yelling to the referee Daggert that there was something on Jersey Joe's gloves. A tough boxing commissioner, Ox De Grossa, who was seated nearby, told Weill to sit down and shut up, and Weill did.

Marciano and his aides believed that liniment on Walcott's upper body was entering Rocky's eyes and burning them whenever he rested his head between the champion's neck and shoulder during a clinch. The fact of the matter was, however, that the damage was being done, unwittingly, in Marciano's own corner, by the application of Dynamite and water.

During the middle rounds, Rocky took a fearful beating. The veteran fight promoter Sam Silverman described it in these words: "Walcott had the legs of a 20-year-old that night. He was having the fight of his career. He must've put Rocky into 200 head-on collisions. It's one of the worst lickings I ever saw a guy take. His corner hit (Marciano) with a sponge full of water and that ran cut stuff into his eyes and blinded him. The poor kid couldn't see. He was getting the shit pounded out of him."

As Jersey Joe pulled steadily ahead on points in the scoring, Rocky sought to summon every shred of determination, guts, killer instinct,

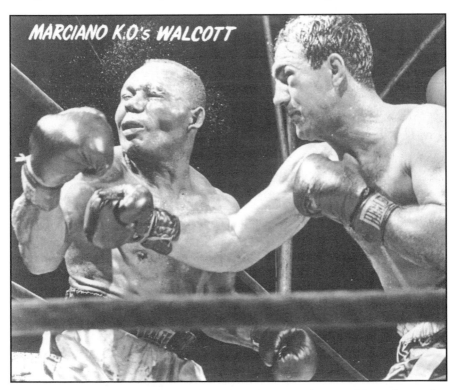

Jersey Joe was planning to throw a left hook when he caught a conclusive short right. (*Hank Kaplan Archives*)

courage—whatever was left in his tank—to win the fight and the title. That he couldn't see straight was something he couldn't worry about.

A Philly boxing writer leaned over and asked Marciano's friend Nicky Sylvester, "What do you think is happening to the youngsta?"

"He's getting his brains beat out," Sylvester replied.

"What'll happen if he loses?"

"I'll tell you what's going to happen: fifty thousand Italians are going to commit suicide in Massachusetts."

By the 10th round, however, Walcott was showing signs of tiring, while the Rock was getting stronger.

"How am I doing?" Rocky asked Colombo.

"Gettin' better," said the cornerman. "Keep after him."

But Walcott amazingly found a second wind. Marciano's body shots should have killed his legs, immobilizing him, but instead the champ continued to move and punch, and his blows were doing damage.

"In the 11th I hit Rocky a body shot I thought would knock him out, but the bell saved him," Walcott said later. "In the 12th it was more of the same. I was covered in his blood, but he kept coming. That Rocky was tough."

"How am I doing?" Rocky asked Colombo again.

"Losin'," said Colombo this time. "You gotta knock him out to win."

This exchange was the turning point, the gateway to the fateful 13th round. The Brockton Blockbuster rose from his corner determined to resolve matters once and for all, to win or lose the fight in this round.

In terms of sheer force of will exerted by a beaten, bleeding, blinded fighter, few performances can match that of Rocky Marciano in Round 13 of this championship fight in September of 1952.

THE 13TH ROUND

Both fighters sensed the importance of this juncture. Both fought as if it were the last round of the fight. Each was intent on knocking out the other. For Rocky it was a must-win round. For Jersey Joe, ahead on points, fighting in his hometown, and with a friendly referee, the preferred tactic would have been to box Marciano and avoid a toe-to-toe shootout. But Walcott was every bit as tough as his adversary, and he was defending his hard-won title. He decided that he would knock out this bloodied, bedraggled challenger.

The round started with Marciano hooking a left to the body. Walcott backed off and retreated to the ropes. It was at this instant that Rocky Marciano threw the punch of a lifetime.

Lou Duva relates what happened. "Jersey Joe was backing up into the ring, setting Marciano up for a left hook. He was going to knock him dead with a left hook, but when he went to lift up his left hand, he couldn't do it. He was paralyzed on that side from all the taps on the shoulder, on the ribs, on the arms. He couldn't manage to throw that left hook, and Rocky just crossed his right hand over Walcott's left side."

It was a jolting, thunderous, short right, which distorted Walcott's entire visage. A famous photograph capturing the impact is still considered one of the most spectacular and revealing depictions of the effect of a perfect punch on the human face. Walcott started to collapse. Marciano, feeling the rhythm of a combination, followed with a looping left hand that missed. It was not needed, however, as Walcott crumpled, one arm looped around the rope and his head on the canvas.

It was over! The title belonged to Marciano. Soon, racists would exult in the ascension of a white man to the throne, while Italians hailed the dominance of one of their own. None of this mattered. Rocky Marciano was heavyweight champion of the world—period.

POSTFIGHT FALLOUT

Sportswriters who had derided Rocky's style as crude and Neanderthal now extracted from their thesaurus some new descriptions: "magnificent animal," "devastating puncher," "inhuman endurance," "courage above the limits of courage," "a bloody but indomitable boxer," and "unstoppable." Now they understood Charley Goldman's succinct description of the fighter: "He ain't pretty, he's just devastatin'."

In the funereal quiet of Jersey Joe's dressing room, the ex-champion lay on a table, sore from head to toe. His cut had been attended to, and finally he spoke in a low, even voice. "I feel the hurt of losing a fight that was so one-sided," he said. "I never felt better or more confident. But, you know what, I was fortunate to have held the title and to lose it to a guy who is a great American."

Walcott's gracious words echoed those of John L. Sullivan when he lost his title in 1892—on a 21st-round knockout—to James J. Corbett in New Orleans.

Naturally, jubilation reigned in the Marciano camp. Rocky's friends, who had won over $50,000 in bets, honored him at a dinner where he was presented with a new Cadillac with license plates that told the story: KO.

AN UNTOLD STORY

The great fight called for a rematch. Every boxing fan clamored for it, but none more desperately than I did. I had a huge personal stake in a Rocky Marciano–Jersey Joe Walcott rematch.

I had enlisted in the air force after spending eight years in college and earning a couple of degrees, including one in the profession of pharmacy. This I thought should entitle me to a commission. Instead, the air force handed me two stripes, denoting the rank of airman second class. To get that commission, my only alternative was Officer Candidate School, for which I qualified in the spring of 1953. The first three months of OCS were sheer hell—the object being to weed out the weaklings and the otherwise unfit.

Part of the intense physical hardship and hazing that the cadets underwent was a rule prohibiting them from smoking, drinking anything but water, and eating candy bars. None of that bothered me, since I did not smoke, drink Cokes, or like candy.

We had a flight officer who was a sports nut. I quickly made a deal with him: If our unit won the championships in an upcoming OCS competition, he would allow us total privacy and lift the ban on smokes and drinks, so that we could watch on television the May 15, 1953, Marciano-Walcott return match for the heavyweight title, to be held in Chicago.

I used this motivation to whip our teams into a kamikaze-like frenzy for the purpose of winning our championships. After all,

A month before his September 14, 1923, fight with Luis Firpo at New York's Polo Grounds, Jack Dempsey (left) posed with his colorful manager-trainer, Jack "Doc" Kearns. (*AP Photo*)

GENE TUNNEY

Art has long been a serious avocation of mine, and boxing champions have been a frequent subject of my paintings. Shown here are my portraits of the 1927 "Long Count" combatants.

Both portraits 1983. Oil on canvas. 48 in. X 30 in. Reproduced from 20 in. X 16 in. lithographs.

JACK DEMPSEY

Max Schmeling chatted with reporters upon his arrival in New York on the ocean liner Berengaria for his 1938 bout with Joe Louis. (*International News Photo/Photofest*)

Schmeling's U.S. sojourn turned sour when Louis decked him in Round 1. (*Hank Kaplan Archives*)

Sugar Ray Robinson, whose career spanned 200 fights over 25 years, trained with Joe Louis for his 1951 showdown in Chicago with Jake LaMotta. (*Associated Press Photo*)

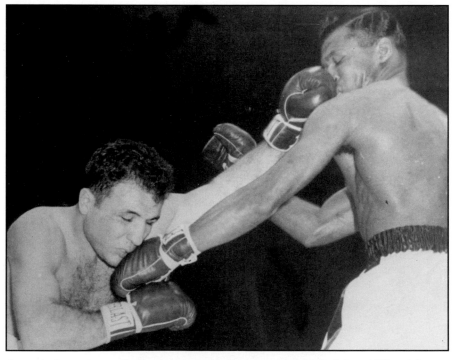

Sugar Ray's training paid off, as he pummeled LaMotta and claimed the middleweight crown. (*Hank Kaplan Archives*)

ROCKY MARCIANO

My rendering of the Brockton Blockbuster, who retired undefeated in 1955. 1983. Oil on canvas. 48 in. X 30 in. Reproduced from a 20 in. X 16 in. lithograph.

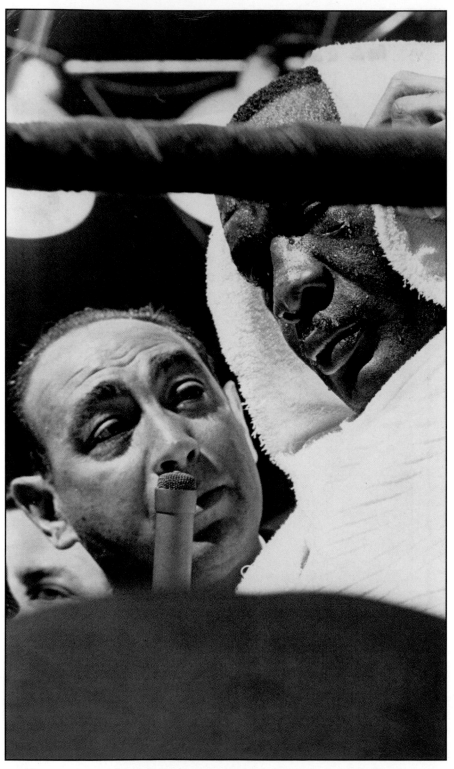

Howard Cosell queried a badly battered Sonny Liston in the wake of Liston's upset loss to upstart Cassius Clay in February 1964 in Miami Beach. (*Hank Kaplan Archives*)

I've spent decades of my life, including the moment captured here, in the company of two historic boxing figures, Muhammad Ali and Don King. (*Photo by Luisita Pacheco*)

African admirers cheered Muhammad Ali during a sightseeing excursion in Kinshasa, Zaire, prior to his Rumble in the Jungle with George Foreman. (*AP Wirephoto*)

That's me on the left, with my longtime cornermates Ali and Bundini Brown.
(*Photo by Luisita Pacheco*)

I reasoned, Marciano and Walcott had fought 13 rounds in their first encounter. This time they would probably go the full 15. Translating that long a bout into minutes and adding time for the prefight and postfight TV coverage meant that we would have at least an hour and a half to smoke, drink Cokes, and eat Hershey bars in an air-conditioned recreation room. After what we'd been going through, no oasis in the Sahara ever seemed as inviting.

We indeed won our championships. Cashing in on the deal I had struck, we were allowed to don comfortable fatigues and slouch around the TV set, smoking, drinking cold Cokes, and munching on Hershey bars.

Of the many millions of Americans who screamed in outrage when Jersey Joe Walcott pitched forward from a perfect right-hand punch after only two minutes and 25 seconds of the first round had expired, none yelled as loudly as the cadets of Charlie Flight, Class of 53C.

"Right! Back in Class A! Formation in front in five minutes, and clean up the mess! Move it! Move it! Move it!" barked our flight officer.

All of a sudden, the upperclassmen swarmed among us like predators on their prey.

Many in my class refused to talk to me for a month after the fight. I can't say I blamed them. It was my introduction to the foolishness of trying to predict the outcome of boxing events.

Who would guess that, years later, I would make a handsome living doing exactly that?

MUHAMMAD ALI VS. ROCKY MARCIANO

Many years after the Marciano-Walcott rematch, I found myself serving as the doctor for an important fight between retired, undefeated heavyweight champion Rocky Marciano and exiled, undefeated heavyweight champion Muhammad Ali.

A Miami television impresario, Murray Woroner, had a vision of matching The Rock with The Lip on a TV soundstage. A computer would be used to write a "script" of how the fight would go, and the boxers would enact the script.

Angelo Dundee would be the cornerman, Chris Dundee the referee, and I the doctor. Why they would need a physician I couldn't guess, but I was happy as a lark to be there.

Rocky, who was in his early 40s, went into training for the "fight" and showed up looking like he was ready to go 15 hard rounds. Vain about his baldness, he even went out and bought a toupee. When he walked into the ring, it sent a chill down my spine. Rocky was ready to go to war.

Across the ring, Ali looked pathetic. During his long layoff, he had treated himself to all the ice cream and cake he could eat, and that was a substantial amount. The tall, slick, slim, perfect body had collapsed into a paunch and a spare tire of flab. Even his handsome face had swollen to moonlike proportions.

The fighters had reversed their roles. Marciano looked like the young fighter; Ali looked positively middle aged! Everyone gasped, but we all treated it as a joke—which, more or less, this event was.

But not to Rocky. His old competitive spirit came surging forth, and Rocky was snorting fire. He argued points in the script. "No, no," he protested. "If Ali threw that jab, I would have nailed him with a right under the heart." Ali would just laugh.

But things got serious when the action moved to the corners of the ring. Marciano was supposed to drive Ali into the ropes, whereupon Ali would punch Marciano with a stinging left jab.

The trouble with this scene was that Marciano was having all kinds of trouble pulling his punches so that they'd miss by inches as Ali was closing with his jab. Again and again one of Rocky's whistling rights would crunch into Ali's ribs, and Ali would wince and look at referee Chris Dundee, seeking help. Chris would smile indulgently and wave the fighters on.

Finally, Ali's good nature could not accept this and he stopped boxing.

"Look, Rock, this is suppose to be play acting. If you keep bombing my ribs, I'm going to have to open up your nose with my real jab," he warned.

Rocky looked apologetic and even said he was, but nevertheless kept landing shots. It began to look like Marciano was goading Ali into a real fight— one real round of all-out war, man to man. Just once, for real.

Chris, Angelo, and I almost fainted at this juicy prospect: an in-shape Rocky Marciano against a badly out-of-shape Muhammad Ali. Oh, brother, what a story!

Murray Woroner saw his golden egg about to be destroyed. He hurriedly stepped in, halting the action, while we all took a long break.

The fight was a joke, a freak show. It had about 15 different endings, depending on which fighter a given audience would want to win. When the tape was shown in Africa, Marciano would lose by a KO, whereas in Italy Ali would bite the dust. In England, Ali would win on a TKO due to cuts. The outcome varied greatly in the States, but guess who won in Dixie?

I watched the fight before a packed house at the Miami Beach Auditorium. In Miami, Ali's home away from home, The Greatest won on a TKO, having inflicted deep cuts all over Rocky's eyes and nose. Marciano was a gory mess, a makeup man's dream.

The audience went wild from the beginning! To this day, I don't know why. It was clearly advertised as a computer-generated fight, but the lack of authenticity didn't matter. The fans went crazy and stayed that way throughout the fight, and when it was over, I was mobbed.

The fans surrounding me wanted to know how long it had taken to sew up Marciano, and would there be a rematch?

As I told this story to Lou Duva, who was seated with me to view the film of Marciano's first KO of Jersey Joe, Lou laughed. "I was with Ali after that computer fight, when both of them came to New York to do the publicity," Lou recalled. "Marciano, like a kid proud of his handiwork, said to me, 'Pick up Ali's shirt, look at his ribs.' I did, and all over Ali's chest, back, and upper belly there's blotches and bumps—all over. And Marciano says to Ali, 'Ali, what happened over there?' Ali says, 'Every time I start to make a little move, he hits me in the ribs, on the arm, in the belly, in the kidneys. Man, he's crazy. He keeps wearing you down. That's what happens when you get in the ring with Marciano.'"

Duva had one more story to tell. He, Marciano, and Joe Louis were walking out of the Miami Beach Auditorium after Cassius Clay had won the heavyweight championship in 1964 from Sonny Liston. Louis had been a big believer in Liston.

Suddenly, Rocky began to jog, slowly pulling away from Joe Louis and Lou Duva.

"Hey, Rock, whatcha doin', where you going?" Louis called after him.

Not slowing down, Rocky said over his shoulder, "Did you hear what that kid got to beat Liston?"

"Naw," said Louis.

"One million dollars," said Rocky, stepping up his pace.

"Wait up," said the Bronx Bomber, jogging after Marciano until they disappeared from view down Washington Avenue, leaving Duva with nothing to do but try to find the nearest ice cream parlor.

If there was one thing Marciano had plenty of, it was self-confidence. At the start of his career, he was severely criticized, made fun of, and dismissed. But there came a point when everything changed in one dramatic moment; when Rocky said, "Yeah, I can be great." Marciano described that moment to Lou Duva.

"Let me tell you one of the stories Rocky told me," says Lou. "When he fought Archie Moore, he got knocked down in the fourth round and the next thing he heard was a count of four. As he started to get up he said to himself, 'I've got to go after this guy. What am I doing on the floor?' Rocky said that is when he knew he was going to be a great fighter. He said, 'When I got up—when I could get up and take a shot, a hard right hand from Archie Moore—then I knew I had it.'"

Angelo Dundee came of age in a boxing world that was ruled by Rocky Marciano. Like all the young veterans who returned to boxing gyms after serving in World War II, Angelo worshipped the champion.

"I saw him grow, I saw him train. I watched the guy that developed him. I know I got a good insight into Marciano," says Angelo.

"Rocky Marciano was the hardest-working heavyweight champion of our era. He retired undefeated. I saw him when he was being developed by a great, great trainer—Charley Goldman, who was one of my teachers—along with Chickie Ferrara. They taught me, and I watched him develop.

"Charley wouldn't train him in Stillman's Gym (in New York)

because Rocky looked so bad at first. He trained at a Catholic Youth Organization gym. I took the subway and went down there. In walks Goldman, wearing coveralls, stoop shouldered, bald headed. He says, 'Angelo, he's got two left feet, but he can punch.' That was the description of Rocky Marciano. I saw him work out that day, and I remember it like yesterday, 'cause I still bum around with Charlie Goldman. In those days we used to go to all the cheap restaurants. I lived on 51st Street and 8th Avenue, right around Jack Dempsey's place. Charley and I were very close, very tight. He was a great trainer."

Rocky Marciano, a gentle, quiet, unassuming family man, a man with the common touch, was clearly the people's champ. His long undefeated streak places him firmly in my pantheon of the great heavyweight champions. Marciano retired with a career record of 49 wins—43 by knockout—and no losses.

Angelo Dundee continues, "I got to know Rocky real well, because he came down here to live in Florida. And I got to know his style. Rocky was very slick. People don't give him credit for being slick. He would take away distance from a guy's jab. One of the regimens of Rocky's training was that Charley would have him bend his knees completely to the floor and come up punching, hitting that heavy bag. He would wind up with a bang! or a bing-bing-bing-boom! and outta there— just like that famous shot he hit Walcott with, which Charley developed and I still remember.

"This guy was so strong. Let's face it, he was undefeated. He was a great fighter."

Cassius Clay, the self-proclaimed Greatest, exulted with cornerman-confidant Drew "Bundini" Brown after vanquishing Sonny Liston and capturing the heavyweight crown. (*Hank Kaplan Archives*)

CASSIUS CLAY vs. SONNY LISTON

CHALLENGER   **CHAMPION**

HEAVYWEIGHT CHAMPIONSHIP

FEBRUARY 24, 1964
MIAMI BEACH

ROUND 5

Political and racial unrest hung heavily in the air of the 1960s. The proposed Civil Rights Act remained to be passed by Congress, the South was still deeply segregated, and racially tinged incidents occurred all over the country. The doctrine of nonviolence espoused by the eloquent Martin Luther King was ignored, resulting in bloody confrontations. In Chicago a tough bunch of black men, dressed in neat black suits and hats, began to strong-arm their way into prominence. They were led by a charismatic, asthmatic ex-con who called himself the Right Honorable Elijah Muhammad and preached black superiority, not racial equality. He advocated separation, not integration. His Black Muslim sect was gaining power when Elijah assigned a fiery, brilliant thinker and speaker, Malcolm X, to the forefront of the movement. Race relations in America were heating up.

CASSIUS AND SONNY

A superstar emerged in the sixties, a man unlike any other in the long history of boxing. Cassius Marcellus Clay was born on January

89

17, 1942, in Louisville, Kentucky, to average lower-middle-class parents. He was an angelic child, according to his sweet, church-lady mother, Odessa. He got involved in boxing because someone had stolen his bicycle. He wanted to administer a good thrashing when he caught up with the thief.

Clay swept through the amateur boxing ranks. He captured the public's admiration and imagination by winning the gold medal at the 1960 Summer Olympics in Rome, exhibiting a loquacious-ness and panache rarely seen in a boxer.

Back in the States, a group of wealthy, white businessmen formed the Louisville Sponsoring Group to underwrite the boxer's nascent career. The group hired the Dundee brothers to direct the boxing progress of the young, charismatic Olympic champion.

The Dundee brothers ran a clean, well-oiled boxing operation that had produced champions. Their headquarters was the 5th Street Gym in Miami Beach, a beehive of boxing activity. Angelo Dundee was the younger brother, brought up in the shadow of his famous sibling Chris, who had managed champions and pro-moted boxing successfully in New York, Miami, and Norfolk, Virginia. The blend of rock-tough, experienced, and Depression-hardened Chris, the promoter; and young, soft-hearted, and end-lessly knowledgeable Angelo, the manager and trainer, made for a great team. Cassius Clay came to Miami to train, and promptly fit into the 5th Street Gym's cast of champions and pugs like fin-gers in a glove.

After one hard look at the tall, laughing, teasing Clay in action in the ring, Chris advised Angelo to pass up a 15-percent share of this fighter's purses and take a weekly salary of $150 instead—which ranks with the sale of Manhattan and the Louisiana Purchase at the top of the list of all-time bad deals.

The 5th Street Gym proved a university for bright, young Cassius Clay. Immediately taken under the wing by two world champions, Clay began to absorb all he saw and adapt it to his own unique talent. But the results often caused the gym's "old gray professors" to laugh openly at him.

"Don't he know he ain't no welterweight?" they'd snort. "He can't move like Luis Rodriguez. He'll be dead tired in three rounds."

They'd go on. "Don't he know he can't pop a jab like Willie Pastrano? Christ, Willie is a light heavyweight. He moves and sticks and moves and sticks. Heavyweights gotta jab like Joe Louis, like Sonny Liston."

And on. "Don't he know he can't hold his hands down by his waist? He can't lean back from a punch. He'll get knocked out in the first bouts."

Only Angelo discerned the magic. A master of developing a fighter according his natural talent, Angelo recognized that he had a phenom on his hands, a heavyweight who moved with the speed of a welterweight and possessed the ring smarts of a master boxer like Willie Pastrano. By turns, Clay boxed with each fighter in the gym, slowly absorbing all their moves like a sponge. Meanwhile, Angelo let Clay be Clay. He didn't try to correct or expunge the young fighter's mistakes; rather, he smoothed them out so that the mistakes worked in Clay's favor.

Years after the "Thrilla in Manila," in which the former Cassius Clay, now named Muhammad Ali, and Joe Frazier staged the greatest fight I ever saw, the esteemed trainer Eddie Futch, Frazier's cornerman in Manila, observed, "Ali takes his mistakes, shows them to you, then beats you with them."

Cassius Clay was a teenager when Angelo installed him in the Mary Elizabeth Hotel, a hellhole of a hostelry located in Miami's Overtown ghetto, known, as I said earlier, as the Swamp.

A miracle occurred there that convinced me that this adolescent boxer was someone special. As the only doctor in the Overtown, I knew how fast the ghetto could destroy a young, impressionable athlete. The lure of booze, drugs, and easy women had made a shambles of many a promising career. But Cassius Clay was different. Somehow he commanded a respect not easily yielded by the "ghetto rats." Everyone deferred to and protected him. I thought, "Boy, if this guy can get these hard, cynical cases to back off, to protect and love him, imagine what he'll do to the American public!"

We launched into a whirlwind tour that would introduce Cassius Clay to the nation. America fell hook, line, and sinker for his act. To add to his charisma, Clay first took to predicting the round in which he would knock out an opponent, then added poetry to his prognostications. It was all childishly simple, but endearingly funny.

It didn't take long to build up a confrontation with the reigning champion, the fearsome Charles "Sonny" Liston. Clay started a campaign to bait Liston into a fight, at one point traveling to Liston's home in Denver, where he awoke Sonny, whom he dubbed "the Bear," in the middle of the night and put a bear trap on his lawn.

Liston was irate. He demanded a fight with this annoying upstart.

Sonny Liston was not a complicated man. He had had a rough, criminal life and worked as an enforcer for the mob. His bosses were Frankie Carbo and Carbo's minion in the boxing world, Blinky Palermo. Liston had served prison time for his criminal activities and been far from an ideal inmate. When he got out of the joint he was a hardened 20-year-old man—huge and thickly built, with an intimidating presence. He had a shotgun jab that was capable of knocking out an opponent, and the early KO was indeed Sonny's MO. He won the heavyweight title by dispatching Floyd Patterson in one round in September 1962, then retained the crown with another first-round KO in their rematch the following year. By the time Cassius Clay signed to fight Sonny Liston, not a boxing writer or other expert could be found who gave Clay even a slim chance. It was a man against a boy, David vs. Goliath, the German army vs. Poland. The consensus: Clay would get himself killed.

Only one expert saw a way for Clay to beat Liston. Luckily, it was the only expert that counted, Angelo Dundee.

Meanwhile, when no one was looking, a fly fell into the ointment.

Despite his fun-filled, freewheeling style, Cassius Clay was a serious young man seeking a principled way through life. Profoundly troubled by the segregation he had experienced growing up, he sought answers for his unsettled mind. His family's Baptist faith provided more questions than answers.

Clay's younger brother Rudy had made the acquaintance of a

man known as Cap'n Sam at Red's barbershop on 10th Street in the Overtown ghetto. Although he didn't make a big deal of it, Cap'n Sam, a.k.a. Sam Saxon, was an ace recruiter for the Black Muslims, the radical separatist religious sect. Conceived in the fertile brain of the Right Honorable Elijah Muhammad, the movement flourished in the penitentiary where he did time. It then grew by leaps and bounds wherever discontented blacks felt they had nowhere else to turn. In such places the Black Muslims offered a safe harbor. They were strict, they were tough and puritanical, and they were all black.

As he was to do throughout his life, Cassius Clay made a choice based on his gut feeling. On the surface, his decision appeared to be exactly wrong for a future heavyweight champion of the world. The Black Muslims received bad press all over America. They were perceived as ex-cons, thugs, and uncompromising religious zealots, just a step removed from the eccentric, suicidal African tribe known as the Fuzzy-Wuzzies. The Muslims were laughed at from afar, but feared from up close. They were becoming a major force and they badly needed a new, improved image. With impeccable timing, into their net fell Cassius Clay, the next heavyweight champion of the world, who had been spending considerable time at Black Muslim rallies.

Angelo and Chris Dundee had scant interest in the rest of the world beyond the realm of boxing and their 5th Street Gym. Neither man had a clue what it meant when, 18 days before the Liston fight, a *Miami Herald* article quoted Cassius Clay Sr. as saying that his son had joined the Black Muslims and henceforth would be known as Muhammad Ali. Cassius Clay was officially dead. Long live Muhammad Ali!

The news exploded like a nuclear device in the promotional offices of Chris Dundee and his partner Bill McDonald, whose money was at risk. Both men were looking forward to counting up a record box-office take and a banner international sale from the upcoming bout. What they had was the setup of a promoter's dreams: a black hat vs. a white hat, villain vs. good guy, man vs. boy, murderer vs. Boy Scout.

Now, with the astounding news that Clay had befriended the Black Muslims, what they had on their hands was a resounding financial catastrophe. The dream matchup had turned into the worst-case scenario: black hat vs. black hat.

Over the next two days incredible pressure was exerted on Malcolm X to save the fight from cancellation. To preserve this once-in-a-lifetime title shot for Clay, Malcolm agreed to leave the supercharged environment of Miami Beach, on the condition that he would return for the fight. Once again, the fight was on!

Charles "Sonny" Liston breathed a sigh of relief. Dressed in his nicest business suit, he took Joe Louis by the arm and got into his limo to ride to the weigh-in. "I only got one worry," Sonny deadpanned. "I might kill this kid."

He had no idea that he was going to lose the fight at the weigh-in.

THE WEIGH-IN

It was February, but it was still hot and humid when 200 newsmen came to see a routine weigh-in. Stars were sprinkled through the crowd. There had never been such interest in a weigh-in.

Backstage, in our dressing room, Angelo Dundee and Clay's idol, Sugar Ray Robinson, were giving their fighter a serious father-to-son talk.

"Son, it's time to get serious. This is for the heavyweight championship of the world," Sugar Ray started in his serene way.

"Yes, sir."

"You gotta stop the high jinks. No poems. No clowning with Bundini Brown." Bundini was Clay's high-spirited cornerman and confidant.

"Yes, sir," promised Clay. He and Bundini looked like schoolchildren receiving instructions from the principal at graduation.

"Go out there, son, like the man you are, the number-one contender."

"Yes, sir."

Okay. All right. Yes. Uh-huh.

And then, as soon as they hit the door of the weigh-in room,

Clay began to chant in unison with Bundini:
"Float like a butterfly,
Sting like a bee,
Rumble, young man, rumble;
Aaagggh!"

The place went wild. Liston, seated at a table and exuding the dignity of a Mafia don, looked on with a bemused expression. Joe Louis looked stunned.

Clay and Bundini danced upon the platform, still chanting. Every once in a while Clay would point to Liston and yell, "I gotcha now, you big ugly bear."

Liston's prefight prophesy that he would win in two rounds proved wrong. (*UPI/Corbis–Bettmann*)

And Liston would smile his heavy-lidded smile and motion for Clay to wait until nighttime, when Liston would flatten him like a pancake.

Finally, after a great confusion on the dais, Clay was brought to the center of the room, where Liston stood. Sonny prided himself on his ability to psyche out his opponent by standing tall and placing towels under his robe so he looked even bigger. He was employing these devices today, but he didn't realize that he was in for a series of shocking surprises.

Clay drew himself up to his full 6-foot-3-inch height and proceeded to look down on Sonny Liston, who was two inches shorter. In person Clay was big, deceptively so. Because he was tall and well-proportioned, he appeared at a glance to be leaner and smaller than he actually was. The fact is, he was bigger than Liston.

The two heavyweights stood there, nose to nose, Liston with a little smile on his face and mayhem in his eyes. Clay was wild-eyed. He tapped Liston's forehead with his fingertips. "I got you now, ol' ugly bear, I got your title now. I'm gonna put a whuppin' on your butt tonight, you big ugly bear!" he recited to a dumb-founded Sonny.

The crowd gasped. Many expected Liston to blow his cool and deck Clay right then and there.

After this outlandish episode, Clay was hustled away to the boxing commission physician, Dr. Alexander Robbins. The doctor found that the fighter's blood pressure had undergone a huge increase, to 210/180. At a loss as to what to do, and unable to find the condition under "Hypertension, heavyweights" in the *Merck Manual* of medical disorders and treatments, Robbins told the press that this finding suggested that Ali was scared to death. If the hypertension persisted at fight time, the bout would be canceled, the physician added.

The doctor's presumptive "diagnosis" actually was prompted by the well-known sportswriter Jimmy Cannon, an acerbic journalist who hated Clay for his different ways. Cannon's champions were Louis and Marciano, quiet, self-effacing men who did their talking in the ring.

Doctor Robbins, the old ring doctor, frankly could not fathom what he was seeing. A huge blood pressure jump; what could it mean? Would he have to cancel an event that half the world was waiting for? Standing nearby, observing the confusion, Cannon offered the doctor an explanation and a way out of his dilemma. "Could it just be that the kid is scared to death?" mused the writer.

"Yes, could be," said the relieved doctor. Newsmen flew to the phones.

"Do you think Clay was nervous or scared?" I later asked Angelo Dundee.

He replied, "I think Clay was feeling like he was going to a party."

As soon as we returned to the house where Clay was staying—which was filled with black-suited, shock-troop Muslims chanting "Death to Whitey!" in unison with a tape recording—I took his blood pressure. It was 120/80; totally normal.

"Why did you do that? Why did you steam yourself up so much that your blood pressure shot up like that?" I asked him.

"I did it to make Liston think that I'm a crazy man," he told me. "See, Liston is a bully, and bullies are scared of crazy people."

Round One to Cassius Clay.

THE FIGHT

The first three rounds of the first Liston-Clay fight were a thing of beauty.

The young Kentuckian was visibly nervous at the start—not scared, but anxious, lest he embarrass himself. He had a plan, which Angelo had dreamed up. Clay would move in circles around Liston, in the style of his sparring partner Luis Rodriguez, and pop a jab à la Willie Pastrano, while studiously avoiding Sonny's slow, hammering jabs. Cassius would lean in and show his face; by the time Liston reacted, Clay would already have pulled back and moved out of range.

Sonny came out sharp. He had trained for a short fight, and

had in fact bet on himself to score a one-round knockout. This incentive caused him to expend a great deal of energy in the first round. He went hard after Clay, but found himself punching air. Clay was on a bicycle. Every once in a while, however, Liston would catch him against the ropes and hurl heavy, pile-driving lefts and rights to his body. Eventually, the boxing theory held, the body would go and the head and legs would follow. Clay believed that the theory didn't apply to him. He could take a hard body shot and kept on ticking. Toward the end of the first round, Clay left his calling card. He stopped moving and whipped a barrage of combinations upon the startled Liston, who hurriedly covered up. Cassius had established himself and his plan: Hit, and not be hit in return; the perfect fight plan.

By the beginning of the fourth round, it was evident that Clay had both the plan and the talent to beat Liston. Sonny's face was

Clay's courage, power, and boxing prowess were vividly on display against Liston. (*Corbis/Bettmann–UPI*)

puffy and speckled with small nicks and cuts from the challenger's snake-lick jabs. His facial tissues were beginning to fall apart. On top of that, he looked confused in his corner between rounds and frustrated in the middle of the ring. Sonny Liston was losing this fight.

Most of Liston's previous fights had been one-sided affairs that ended early. He hadn't had to learn the art of cutting off a running opponent. Perhaps tonight he would pay the price for this oversight.

But suddenly the fight took a bizarre turn. But for Angelo Dundee's expertise in his corner, Clay would have quit, lost the fight, and been laughed out of boxing.

Returning to his corner, Cassius reported that his eyes were burning. He could not see.

"Cut 'em off! Cut my gloves off!" he wailed, his eyes stinging and tears streaming down his cheeks. "I knew they'd fix this fight. They told me the gangsters would fix this fight."

Liston's mob connections, which he couldn't be bothered to hide, had frightened the Muslims, who were in over their heads with their involvement in this event. Their paranoia reached the extreme point of suspecting Angelo (who is Italian) and me (Spanish) of being influenced by the Mafia.

The prevailing thought among the Muslim muscle was that Angelo had deliberately put an irritating substance into Clay's eyes. If the fight should have to be stopped, Angelo would pay a stiff price—a severe beating, or maybe even his life.

Meanwhile, in Clay's corner Angelo Dundee was proving why he is the greatest cornerman in the world. While washing out his fighter's eyes as best he could, he kept up a steady, reassuring chatter. "You can't quit now, son. This is for the heavyweight championship of the world. This is what we been working for. Stand up, son," he counseled.

The referee, Barney Felix, noticing this commotion, started toward the corner to investigate. Angelo, spotting his movement, stood Clay up, forcing him to move his legs. Felix, satisfied that nothing was amiss, retreated to await the bell for the fifth round. The first major obstacle on what would be the future Muhammad Ali's road to immorality had been skirted.

Later, watching those machinations in the corner unfold on film, I posed a question to Angelo, who was seated beside me: "Did you recognize that you saved Ali's career with your great corner work and by putting him out there again to fight an animal like Liston when he couldn't see him?"

Angelo, the most modest of boxing men, said, "Coulda, shoulda, woulda. That's what you're there for. Thank God I was there and made the right decision."

But was Clay's blinding intentional? Did Liston's corner apply something illicit to Sonny's gloves? Or did they merely rub oil of wintergreen on his sore shoulder, with the result that some of the oil was transferred to Clay's forehead in a clinch and then dripped into his eye?

Says Angelo, "I didn't wear specs then. I put my finger in the corner of his eye and then put it in my eye, and there was definitely a caustic substance in there. So I'm trying to get it out. I got the sponge, went through both of his eyes, wiped them clean with a towel, and threw the sponge and towel away because I didn't want them around with that substance on them. I knew there was something in his eye. He kept telling me, 'Cut the gloves off, cut the gloves off.' He wanted to prove to the world that there was dirty work afoot. I said to him, 'Bullshit, this is for the title.' Then the referee was coming toward my corner. I made Clay stand up. I didn't pick him up; I said, 'Stand up, stand up!' He wanted to go towards the referee, but I pulled him back because, you know, if a guy goes to the referee shaking his head, wanting to have his gloves cut off, the ref stops the fight."

Clay was blinded. His eye burned painfully. His hands were encased in gloves, so he could not perform the natural act of wiping his burning, tearing eyes. Only 60 seconds remained before the bell would sound to begin Round 5—not enough time for even a great cornerman like Angelo Dundee to rectify the problem. Angelo had come to love Clay like a son. Now he was faced with the hardest decision imaginable: whether to send his fighter back out, blind as he was, to face an enraged killer. Liston was accustomed to inflicting serious damage on other men. In comparison, Clay was like a boy, but tonight the boy was beating the man. Even the cynical reporters on hand had to admit that Clay had apparently found the formula for beating tough Sonny Liston. He was indeed on the way to winning this fight.

What choice would Angelo make?

"All I did was give him the perfect instruction—'run'—and that is what he did," says Angelo. "He ran and, thankfully, the dear Lord came into play: tear ducts cleaned (Clay's) eyes and he proceeded to kick the heck out of the other guy."

Teddy Atlas, the brilliant young trainer, manager, and cornerman, who also is a boxing commentator on TV, joined us in the television studio and offered his perspective on the choice that faced Angelo that night.

"In that position, obviously you have a responsibility to be safe; a responsibility to make the right decisions to safeguard the health of the fighter," says Atlas. "But you also have a responsibility to make sure you do everything to win. And, whether you're coaching a football or basketball game or working the corner for a boxer, you have to remember that the situation can change, and you don't want to panic.

"You want to look at the landscape. What you decide to do depends on what has been going on; in this case, how Liston had been dealing with Ali's style up to that point. What was important and, I'm sure, what Dundee was looking at, was how the quickness of Ali didn't allow Liston to get into range where he could make it a slugfest. It wasn't like Liston was landing punches. He was being frustrated by Ali's speed. Under those conditions—Ali wasn't letting Liston get close to him—he could take a little bit of a chance. Dundee could afford to say, 'Hey, let me buy a round here. Let me send this guy out because the other guy hasn't been able to get close to my man.' It is not like this was the Thrilla in Manila. It's not like Ali was taking shots from Frazier. Liston wasn't getting close to him. So, under those circumstances, I think history obviously tells you that (Dundee) made the right choice."

THE UNTOLD STORY

In my opinion, the finest, most complete, and most honest biography of Ali is Thomas Hauser's *Muhammad Ali: His Life and Times*. In a conversation with me, Hauser shed some new light on this controversy.

"Of course, one of the issues surrounding this fight is whether or not there was some intentional act that caused temporary blindness," said Hauser. "If you go back in Liston's career, Sonny won a 12-round decision over Eddie Machen in 1960. After the fight, Machen complained in the locker room that he couldn't see, that he had been temporarily blinded. But he had fought such a lousy fight that nobody paid any attention to him. A year earlier, Liston had fought Cleveland Williams. Williams gave him a terrific fight in the first round. He was still pretty tough in the second round, but then he got knocked out in the third round. Afterward, in the dressing room, Williams was blinking and said he had a lot of trouble seeing.

"So this wasn't the first time that something like this happened to a Sonny Liston opponent. Jack McKinney, a very good boxing writer out of Philadelphia, said that years after this fight with Ali, one of Liston's cornermen told him that if he watched the tape of the fight, he'd see that before the fourth round, one of the men in Liston's corner is bending down; you can't see what he's doing, but he's doing something with Sonny's gloves," said Hauser.

"This was one moment where Angelo really was an inspired genius between rounds. He saved Muhammad Ali's career because, given the social and political climate of the time, if Cassius Clay quits, he loses the fight; he never becomes Muhammad Ali; he never gets another chance to fight for the championship; and boxing history, maybe even world history, turns out differently."

Meanwhile, Teddy Atlas's eyes were glued to the television monitor as we ran the tape over and over. It was Atlas's first prolonged viewing of the "Blind Round," and as he watched it he provided a cornerman's professional analysis:

"Ali's just trying to stay away from the man. He turns Liston so he can continue to have an escape route. This is why Angelo Dundee made the decision to let him go back out—because he has legs. If he was going to walk in and just stand in front of Liston, maybe Dundee has to make a different, difficult choice.

"One of the things that saved Ali was that as his career went on, he reinvented himself. He was able to reinvent and show diversity by changing his style to what suited the style of the man in front of him. When he had to use his legs, he used his legs. If he had to go on the ropes—when he didn't have his legs anymore and he had to block and break a guy down psychologically, which is what he did in the Foreman fight—he was able to adapt to that.

"Like Cus D'Amato used to say to me, in the first part of Ali's career, the only time you touched Ali is when the referee made you touch gloves before the bout started."

Clay prevailed over blurred vision and some solid early shots from Sonny.
(*Corbis/Bettmann–UPI*)

CLAY'S GREAT ESCAPE

Round 5 was terrifying for Clay and his camp. He could not see Liston. His eyes burned like fire and his nose ran; his pain was incessant.

At first, Liston did not understand what was happening. Then, slowly, it dawned on him that Clay was giving way and starting to run. This kind of running wasn't Clay's graceful glide, but was more like a hasty retreat. Encouraged, Liston pressed his attack. Swinging wide, powerful left hooks, he tried to find the range, but Clay, rubbing his eyes, remained just beyond the punches' reach. Occasionally, however, the challenger was forced to grab Liston in a clinch, whereupon Sonny would launch a barrage of body-killing shots. Cassius winced, but held on. Liston stepped up the pace of his onslaught, but his misses were wild, he was tiring noticeably, and one of his shoulders seemed to be hurting.

Clay's face showed no sign of fear, and although he rubbed his eyes repeatedly with his gloves, Liston didn't seem to get the message that his opponent was vulnerable. Sonny pressed forward, missing badly with most of his powerful, wide-arcing hooks. Later, some of his supporters would maintain that all these big misses had injured Liston's shoulder. They might have hurt Sonny, but they assuredly didn't hurt Clay.

By midround Clay's eyes had improved, and he devised a new tactic. He would place his left glove on Sonny's forehead and leave it there. Then, after a moment had passed, he would tap Sonny lightly four or five times, thus diverting him from his attack. The maneuver enraged Liston, but he didn't seem to know what to do about it.

Clay had also come up with another annoying tactic: grabbing the back of Liston's head and drawing him forward into a clinch whenever Sonny got too close to him. This is totally illegal, but referee Felix was as baffled by the move as Liston, and Clay got away with it.

With just 30 seconds left in the round, Clay's eyes had cleared and he knew that he had survived the bout of blindness. He had passed his sternest test, and in the fire of the challenge his character had been forged. Later in his career, he would fight an entire bout against Ken Norton with a broken jaw, and no one would be surprised. After all, this man had faced down an enraged killer that he couldn't even see clearly, so what was the big deal about a fractured jaw?

Now Clay's confidence was growing by the second. He began to throw and land crisp shots. Sonny, meanwhile, looked exhausted. Cassius leapt to the attack and rained punches on Liston. The bell rang, ending the round. One more round would be fought, but every boxing man present knew that this fight was already over.

AFTERMATH

Sonny Liston quit in his corner before the start of the seventh. His cornermen claimed a shoulder injury. His face was puffy and cut up. He was a beaten fighter, sitting sullenly on his stool, trying to figure out what had gone wrong. Willie Reddish, his chief second, said, "It's OK. There'll be another night." But there never really would be another night for Sonny Liston.

Clay ran crazily around the ring, screaming at the gathered press and fans. The night was his. This was the first big step for the fighter who would call himself The Greatest and back up that boast. "I told you! I told you! I shocked and amazed the world! I am the greatest!" he exulted.

This fight not only made the future Muhammad Ali a champion; it displayed to the world the man's moral fiber and strength of character. In fighting a killer like Liston while blind, Clay had vividly demonstrated his courage, determination, competitiveness, and ability to withstand pain. He had also made it clear that, no matter what the circumstance, he would never quit. Finally, by throwing an apparently hysterical fit at the weigh-in, he had devised a brilliant psychological ploy that would again prove to be a deciding factor in his next fight with Liston.

After the fight was over, when I had come down from the high that night produced, I realized that Clay had turned a corner; that in the most concrete sense, this fight would be the keystone of his career. He had gone from being a freak attraction to the legitimate heavyweight champion of what he always called "the whole wide world."

Says Thomas Hauser, "Without this fight there is no Muhammad Ali, because he was basically regarded as an entertainer, a curiosity, up to this point. Most people didn't really take him seriously as a fighter, some even after he won this fight. There were rumors that the fight was fixed. Liston implied that he hadn't trained properly for it. One of the reasons that you had such a circus in the second fight, with Ali standing over Sonny Liston, screaming for him to get up and refusing to go to a neutral corner, was that Ali wanted to prove that the first time hadn't been a fix, hadn't been a fluke."

PACHECO'S LOSS: AN UNTOLD STORY

This fight was by far the biggest win I had experienced since I started working in the corners as a fight doctor for Angelo and Chris Dundee in 1960. But it was also my biggest loss—a debacle—in a financial sense.

From the time boxing matches first appeared on television, I had supplemented my money in college by keeping up with boxers. A fraternity house in the Deep South was an easy place to win a quarter bet. All you had to say was, "I'll take the black guy." If the opponent was white, you had a bet. Of course the "black guy" was usually Sugar Ray Robinson, Archie Moore, Ezzard Charles, or Jersey Joe Walcott, which is to say, easy money.

Until I became professionally involved in boxing, I kept on betting. The amounts got bigger as my income increased. It seemed a very easy way to make money; after all, I was the doctor for all of the fighters at the 5th Street Gym, and knew the condition of every one of them.

My then wife's best friend was a stunningly beautiful Vegas showgirl called Charlotta Divine, who had married America's number-one sports handicapper. He was so good that he set the betting line or point spread on baseball, football, and basketball games and boxing matches. His name was Bob Martin, and he was wonderful to be around. A gang of bookies hung around him in a kind of Guys and Dolls cluster, always talking bets and sports.

Bob Martin knew boxing better than any man I've ever run across. He would make any newspaper scribe or radio or TV expert look like an amateur.

"Bet this kid every fight until he loses," Bob would say. As if that were not enough, he'd add, "And Angelo has a Cuban, Ultiminio 'Sugar' Ramos. Bet him every time until he loses, too."

A maitre d' at the Alexandria Hotel in L.A. overheard us once and did just that. Today he lives in a great beach house in Malibu and owns three Mercedes cars.

My story for the Clay fight with Liston has the opposite ending, unfortunately.

Drew "Bundini" Brown and Solomon McTier, our two cornermen for the Liston fight, came to my Overtown office in Miami's ghetto before the bout. Each brought a $100 bill. They wanted to bet on Clay at 7 to 1. I had saved $5,000 to put on Clay myself, but I felt that the price might go to 9 to 1, so I told the guys I'd wait until fight time to see if we could get even better odds. I put their two $100 bills in my wallet.

As we know, the weigh-in became a near-riot, with Clay going crazy, Bundini yelling and screaming, and Clay's blood pressure apparently rising to 210/180 or even higher. His pulse was astronomical. Dr. Robbins didn't know what to do. With over 200 press credentials issued, the fight couldn't realistically be canceled. It was a nightmare.

It was agreed that I would stay with Clay all day and monitor his blood pressure hourly, keeping an accurate chart, in the event that a decision might be made that would occasion a lawsuit.

As mentioned, Clay's little house was packed with hard-core Nation of Islam storm troopers, some of whom were serving as bodyguards for the fighter. They spent their time listening to those "Kill Whitey!" tapes. Angelo and I were the only two "whiteys" in the house, so we followed some classic Bob Martin advice, "Act as if." In this case we acted as if we were black.

Clay's blood pressure dropped to 120/80 in the limo on the way to the auditorium. He seemed unruffled, as if he knew his blood pressure would not be a problem.

"Now the big ugly bear thinks I'm crazy! Bullies are scared of crazy people," he observed, and every head in the limo nodded.

Cassius seemed to view the whole occasion as a huge joke. If it was a joke, it provided him a huge psychological advantage. Sonny was convinced that Clay was crazy, and that concerned him.

As fight time approached, our group drove over to the Miami Beach Auditorium. In the limo's front seat, the two Muslim bodyguards kept playing that "Kill Whitey!" tape. Angelo and I didn't say much.

Arriving at the auditorium, we repaired to our dressing room. After fighting in one of the preliminary bouts, Clay's brother Rudy (who later took the first name Rahman), who was also a boxer, joined us and assumed the important task of "watching" the drinking water so that no one could "poison" it. After all, Angelo was an Italian and, therefore, undoubtedly a member of the Mafia. The Muslims thought I was Italian, too, although I am Spanish. Hysteria and paranoia ran high in that little room. Time and again Cassius caught his brother looking away, neglecting his duty, and time and again he made him change the water.

Finally, it was time to go. Time to Shock 'n' Amaze the Whole Wide World! Time for the world to acknowledge that Cassius Clay was The Greatest!

And so he proved to be! Joyous was the celebration in the ring. We laughed, we cried, we hugged each other, until Bundini said to me, "We rich, Doc! When can I get my 800 bucks?"

And then it hit me! For every moment of this day I had been tied up with Clay, so I hadn't had a chance to bet the money for Bundini and Solomon—or for me! Not getting the bets down cost me big. I lost $1,400 out of my pocket—I had to pay Bundini and Solomon the $700 each would have won— and I failed to win the $35,000 that I would have collected from Bob Martin on my $5,000 bet at 7 to 1. At the time, that represented the balance of my home mortgage. Life with Cassius Clay/Muhammad Ali was always filled with surprises!

So The Greatest won, but I lost. What's worse, it wouldn't be the last time this happened.

The combatants exchanged solemn stares prior to their rematch in Lewiston.
(*AP Wirephoto*)

MUHAMMAD ALI vs. SONNY LISTON
CHAMPION   CHALLENGER

HEAVYWEIGHT CHAMPIONSHIP

MAY 25, 1965
LEWISTON, MAINE

ROUND 1

By the mid-sixties, much of the world was in upheaval. Signs of political and social change were ubiquitous. Rejecting the peaceful ennui of the 'safe' fifties, teenagers fled their orderly, suburban, middle-class lives and rebelled openly against an escalating war and the values of their parents' generation. The world was filled with a new music, provided by the Beatles, and excited by a new boxing champion who was another child of the rebellion: the young, handsome hero Muhammad Ali. Smoke was in the air. Some of it came from shared marijuana joints and pipes, some from burning cities torched by rioters, and some from the guns of assassins.

The spirit of revolution was abroad in the land. American youth, fueled by idealism born of affluence, wanted control. This was the baby boom generation, and it was coming of age.

As Muhammad Ali prepared to travel to Maine for his rematch with Sonny Liston, the nation's new president, Lyndon B. Johnson, announced an antipoverty program he called the Great Society. He also signed into law the sweeping Voting Rights Act and, sadly, sank deeper into the quagmire of Vietnam. He expanded American

111

involvement in the war, driving some alienated youths to burn draft cards, incinerate the flag, and flee to Canada.

Ali was to leave his mark on this decade when he refused induction into the army, saying, "I ain't got nothing against them Vietcong." He faced a prison term and the loss of his hard-won title, but he held fast to his principles. In the end he won, emerging as a hero with a reputation far grander than any he might have earned simply as the heavyweight champion of the world.

Muhammad Ali, the personality, had arrived.

THE PREFIGHT HYPE

If ever there was a man who wanted to relive a bad moment in order to correct a mistake and obtain vindication, that man was Charles "Sonny" Liston. Liston had fallen from his high perch as "the baddest man on the planet" and been exposed as an aging, confused fighter and, worse, a quitter. The public estimation of him hovered near zero. Liston had been made a joke by a brash, loudmouthed kid.

This transformation did not sit well with Sonny. As soon as the contract for a rematch, to be held in Boston, had been signed, he went into serious training. The boxing crowd was surprised to see the diligence with which he went about his training. Come fight night, he vowed, the real Sonny Liston would appear once again, prepared to go the distance if necessary.

But Ali had plenty of one thing that Sonny had little of, and that was luck. Muhammad Ali had lived a charmed life. Liston's life—a chronicle of violence, imprisonment, and, at the end, drug addiction—had been anything but charmed. Now, just when Sonny Liston had got himself as ready as he could be for his chance at redemption, bad luck tapped him on the shoulder again.

On the night of Friday, November 13, 1964, three days before the big rematch, Ali was watching TV in his suite in the Sherry Biltmore Hotel in Boston when he was overcome by a sudden wave of nausea that was followed by vomiting. He was rushed to a nearby hospital, where he was diagnosed as having an incarcerated inguinal hernia. He was transferred to Boston City Hospital and underwent a 70-minute operation.

Back in Liston's camp, a curtain of gloom descended. The fight would have to be postponed for six months. Could an old fighter—Sonny was born in 1932, according to him; in 1929, according to others—endure a rigorous training regimen all over again? Liston had honed an "edge" and was ready to kill in November, but how could he preserve that physical and mental edge for six more months? Once again, Sonny's chronic bad luck had tapped him on the shoulder at a most inconvenient time.

The press coverage surrounding the fight was feverish. The media had a field day with the Ali-Liston rivalry and, by extension, the groups behind the fighters: on one side the Mafia family, led by Frankie Carbo and Blinky Palermo, who were said to "own" Liston; and on the other side the ominous Nation of Islam, which, the press alleged, had ordered the February 21, 1965, assassination of Malcolm X. Malcolm had severed his ties with the Nation of Islam in order to form a new religious sect, whose philosophy was less separatist and more conciliatory toward white society, a position that Elijah Muhammad roundly condemned.

Following soon after the assassination of the charismatic Malcolm X came the news that the state of Massachusetts had refused to sanction the bout. Between Liston's Mafia connections and an escalating internecine war in the Muslim nation, the Bay State's leadership felt that the combatants should move their show elsewhere.

In spite of the swirling rumors of impending violence and bloodshed, the unlikely state of Maine announced that it would sanction and welcome the star-crossed match. The fight would be held on May 25, 1965, at St. Dominic's Arena—a small youth center in Lewiston, Maine.

Any dangers surrounding the fight had been blown wildly out of proportion by the hysterical press. As a result, Maine state police began planning roadblocks that would intercept unsavory characters before they could reach Lewiston. Such measures had the effect, of course, of killing the gate for the fight.

The irony of all the parochial shenanigans was hardly lost on the boxing mavens. In any other setting and without the extracurricular distractions, this Ali-Liston rematch would go through the box-office roof, perhaps becoming the biggest-grossing fight in history.

But if the endless prefight distractions and hysteria were a disappointment to serious boxing fans, this sideshow was nothing compared to what was in store for them when the bell sounded to start Round 1 of Ali-Liston II.

THE FIGHT

The crowd was sparse, the atmosphere tense; over all, this fight had an otherworldly quality. The audience seemed to include more security people, from FBI agents to local law enforcement types in streetclothes, than fight fans.

Ali seemed oblivious to the pressure-packed atmosphere, dancing out lightly as the bell sounded for Round 1. Liston, scowling, advanced with a determined, killer stare. Referee Jersey Joe Walcott, the former heavyweight champ, shadowed the fighters as they circled warily. Liston had trained long and hard, focusing on cutting off the ring on Ali. His downfall in the first fight was due mostly to his inability to cut off the ring. There were other factors for Sonny to ponder. He had always depended on his thunderous body attack to slow down an opponent. With Ali he received two nasty surprises: first, it was difficult to hit Ali with a hard body shot; second, and more discouraging, Ali could absorb a strong body attack without noticeable effect.

In the round's opening minute Ali circled right, lightly flicking his snake-lick jab. Sonny, in grim pursuit, punched mainly the air, missing his target as he had in the first fight. This time, however, Liston seemed to have adjusted, at least for the early rounds. His plan was to pound the body, cut off Ali, and hope for an opening for his devastating left jab or right cross. By the middle rounds Ali would tire, come down off his toes, and park his bicycle. Then Sonny Liston would take command and batter the kid into submission. Such was the plan, and it was a good one, except for one thing: Ali had a better plan.

At the start the first round, Ali delivered a wake-up call in the form of a hard right that landed flush on Sonny's jaw. Ali surprised many opponents in this way; the popular wisdom held that he couldn't punch, but he could. The hard right woke up Liston. He continued to chase Ali, but with a discernible dollop of caution.

A minute later, Ali stopped, planted his feet, and let fly a stunning right hand. Liston blinked. He had felt it. Ali now began toying with Sonny, drawing him into a clinch by placing his glove behind Liston's head and pulling. Referee Walcott ignored this illegal maneuver. Liston was frustrated and mad. He intensified his pursuit. He landed a few thumping body shots, but nothing significant.

Ali was using the ropes beautifully to avoid being cut off in the corners. As Ali's back grazed the ropes, Sonny jabbed and missed. Ali threw a hard right hand over the errant jab, gaining leverage and speed from the slingshot effect produced by coming off the ropes as he threw the punch. Pivoting on his right foot, using the ropes for power and propulsion, Ali exploded the quick right high on Liston's head.

Sonny's left foot lifted involuntarily with the impact of the blow. Now Sonny crumpled, falling heavily to the canvas. He tried to get up reflexively, but then rolled over, unable to recover his coordination.

At this point, we must digress for a moment. The right hand off the ropes was a favorite Ali technique, which he loved to use in the gym and in the ring. The punch with which he had just hit Liston had speed and steam behind it, but the blow had eluded the notice of many ringside observers, causing confusion and some outrage among the fans and reporters. "Did you see a punch?" they asked one another, shaking their heads.

Liston fell over onto his back. Ali stood motionless for a moment, in disbelief. Why was Liston still down? Ali seemed to be asking himself. He hovered above Liston like a matador over a fallen bull. Waving his glove, he demanded that Liston get off the canvas. "Get up, you bum!" Ali screamed. "Nobody's going to believe this. Get up!"

Walcott, caught off guard by the punch and Liston's reaction to it, went over to where Liston lay. Jersey Joe seemed confused. He looked at the timekeeper, who also seemed paralyzed with indecision. Walcott then motioned for Ali to go to a neutral corner. Ali took off on a circular trot around the ring, jumping up and down and whooping. Walcott then seemed to insist to Liston that he get up; Ali, meanwhile, continued to run around in circles. Liston rose feebly to one knee, failed to gain his balance, and rolled over onto his back.

THE UNTOLD STORY

I sought out Mills Lane, the nonpareil modern-day referee, for his opinion, since, as we shall see, this disastrous fight was mainly the result of poor refereeing. Mills has been a boxer, marine, cowboy, prosecuting criminal attorney, state's attorney, and district court judge. These qualifications explain why he has been called the best referee ever. Mills expressed doubt about the sincerity of Liston's reaction to Ali's punch.

Says Mills, "I think it was a legitimate knockdown. But I do not believe it was a legitimate enough punch to have knocked him out. Liston did some acting, and I also think Liston figured he couldn't beat Ali and, thinking that he was going to get beat again, he looked for a way to get out of there."

Here's Angelo Dundee's take: "Perfect move, just like I teach my fighters: hit the guy on top of the head. If you look at this *Sports Illustrated* magazine, (the photo) shows (Liston's) left hook picking up the force of the blow. He definitely got nailed. He didn't expect the punch."

Also present for our conversation was Emanuel Steward, who is widely regarded as one of the brainiest men in boxing. He offered a different perspective on the questionable knockdown.

"Sonny Liston was in great fear of the Black Muslims, who were a very powerful and intimidating force at that time," says Emanuel. "I think the fact that he had been threatened by the Black Muslims had a big effect on him. In addition, he was afraid of Ali because Ali was crazy or whatever.

"I believe that Sonny was acting to a great degree. I think the punch was a good punch because Ali was a specialist in that particular punch, but I think that Ali himself didn't believe that it was hard enough to knock out Sonny Liston."

Angelo Dundee adds this thought: "Ali had Liston convinced that he was a nut case, so Liston stayed down. Thank God he stayed down. He was getting up, you know, hesitantly, 'cause he didn't want to get up and face that nut."

Back in the ring, Liston remained on his back, refusing to get up; Ali was running around, taunting Sonny and exhorting him to rise; and Jersey Joe Walcott and the timekeeper were both mired hopelessly in a fog of indecision and confusion, with no end in sight.

When Liston hit the canvas, it was Walcott's duty to wave Ali to a neutral corner before he began a count over Liston. This is the same rule—the neutral-corner rule—that brought about the Long Count in the Dempsey-Tunney fight.

Suddenly, out of the stands came a wizened, 79-year-old man with a stopwatch in his hand. This old guy was yelling that the fight was over because 17 seconds had elapsed since Liston was knocked down. Was this little old man a member of the boxing commission, or some other important official? No, he was Nat Fleischer, the well-known editor and publisher of *The Ring* magazine. He wasn't a boxing commissioner, but he carried a lot of weight in boxing circles.

Walcott, in the absence of a better plan, stopped the fight. There was just one problem: by this time Liston had gotten up and the fight had resumed! Ali was showering punches on Liston, who was desperately trying to cover up. The crowd was roaring in disbelief. Finally, Walcott interceded and stopped the fight, declaring Ali the winner by a knockout in the first round. No one was brave enough to announce an official time for the KO.

Angelo Dundee, who at the time was as bewildered as anyone else by the strange doings in the ring, has this to say: "Nat Fleischer, thank

God, was seated on the right-hand side of me, with the guy who was the timekeeper. In fact, I thought they had hired Nat Fleischer as the timekeeper. I yelled over to Nat when the count reached 10. I said, 'Call Joe. Fight's over!'"

One of the worst mistakes a boxing commission can make is to appoint a former boxing champion as the referee for an important match. Apart from the principals, the referee is the most important man at a fight. Life-and-death decisions affecting the fighters are in his hands. Only professional referees should be allowed to officiate. Period. Not Joe Louis, and certainly not Jersey Joe Walcott. On this night in Lewiston, Maine, Walcott was in over his head.

"The fact that you were a fighter would not necessarily make you a great referee, but even if it will help, you have to have some training, some experience," says Mills Lane. "That was a terrible appointment (for this Ali-Liston fight). Going in, you've got a problem. Walcott didn't know what to do. He made some terrible mistakes, and it's obvious. Walcott might have been a great fighter, but he was a terrible referee. He should not have listened to Nat Fleischer, who was out of line for injecting himself into the situation. Finally, what happened was a complete travesty."

Mills continues: "Here is what happens. Liston goes down. Once he is on the deck, the timekeeper starts. Now, the referee's initial job, once he sees that a guy is down, is to get the fighter who scored the knockdown in a neutral corner. I tell the fighters in the dressing rooms before the fight, 'If you score a knockdown, go to the farthest neutral corner as quickly as you can. If you delay getting there, I will not pick up the count. The timekeeper might tell me the count is at six, but I will pick it up at two. As the referee, you penalize the four seconds it took you to get the fighter to a neutral corner. By not going to a neutral corner and staying there, a fighter is effectively penalizing himself.

"So, if Ali comes out of the corner and runs around like he did, you wave the count off. You put him back in the corner and resume the count where you left off. Walcott didn't do that. You can see Walcott looking at Liston while Ali is running around, then looking over at somebody who was apparently talking to him, and Ali is still running around. Walcott should have stopped the action, taken Ali back to the corner, and then gone back and picked the count up."

Precious seconds ticked off the clock, with no count proceeding, while Walcott chased the prancing Ali as Liston lay inert on the canvas. Another question arises: At what point should a referee, having lost patience, disqualify a fighter who refuses to go to or remain in a neutral corner?

Mills Lane, a strict disciplinarian in the ring, explains, "That is why you go to the dressing rooms before the fight and tell the fighters and the chief seconds what the protocol is. Now, in the ring you try to give a guy some slack. In this case I would have taken Ali back to a neutral corner. If he had left the corner a second time, I would have told him that if he did it again he was gone, disqualified."

So if an experienced, gutsy referee had been working this fight, is it possible that Ali would have been disqualified and Sonny Liston would have recaptured the heavyweight championship while floundering on the floor like a beached whale? I ask Mills.

"It is possible," Lane replies.

Mills pauses, recalling the bizarre events surrounding that fight. "I tell you, for all his wildness in those days, Ali was electric. He was crazy like a fox when he fought. Later, his craziness was controlled. He knew what he was doing. But in this fight he was really like an excited kid. Angelo should have grabbed him and might have controlled him, but Walcott never walked him over to a neutral corner. He never did anything. This was a complete botch job from beginning to end, starting with the making of the fight.

"They should have called the fight off—before it happened. When they talk about Muslims and Mafia and blocking the roads to Lewiston, Maine, who ever heard of such nonsense? That was mostly the result of the press's trying to build a story. Has anyone ever seen roadblocks to a heavyweight championship? Roadblocks chase people away. They should have said time out, stop the fight, and Ali would have defended his title six months later in the Garden, in Las Vegas, in Miami, with proper officials in charge. That would have been, in the end, the proper thing to do, and much more profitable."

SONNY ON THE STAND

The entire audience in Lewiston had been stunned by the sudden stoppage of the fight. What was happening? The boxers were fighting hard, so why stop the fight?

But as we know, it was stopped. Afterward, Ali was running around the ring, arms outstretched, telling one and all that he was indeed The Greatest, as he never tired of repeating.

Then a television monitor was brought into the ring, and the round was replayed as Ali narrated it. He was in midsentence when Sonny suddenly plummeted to the canvas. Nonplussed at missing the sight of his own knockdown punch, Ali, without missing a beat, said, "I was so fast, even I missed seeing the punch."

A few years later, I was attending a California Boxing Commission meeting with Howard Cosell. The matter before the commission was the reinstatement of Sonny Liston, whose boxing license had been suspended after the Lewiston debacle.

Liston was dressed in a beautiful suit and accompanied by a smooth, refined attorney who opened the hearing with a statement replete with "wherefores" and "notwithstandings." Having heard enough of that, Sonny waved to him to shut up, growling, "Cut the bullshit; let 'em ask what they want."

The hearing immediately focused on what the commission referred to, distressingly, as "the fixed fight."

Sonny nodded, understanding fully that they were asking about the Phantom Punch. Obligingly, he picked up the story right at what must be called its punch line.

"Ali knocked me down with a sharp punch," he testified. "I didn't see it, and I went down, but I wasn't really hurt. Then I saw Ali standing over me, yelling like a nut.

"Now there is no way to get up from the canvas and not be exposed to a great shot. Ali is waiting to hit me. The ref, Walcott, can't control him. I have to put one glove on the canvas and get up on one knee."

Liston climbed down from the witness stand and demonstrated. We all leaned forward to see the Bear on the floor.

"See, as soon as there is daylight between my knee and the canvas, Ali can hit me," Sonny continued.

Then he stood up, straightened his suit, and, with an earnest look on his face, said with obvious sincerity, "And you all know Ali is a nut—you can tell what a normal man is going to do, but you can never tell what a nut is going to do."

By and large, until his death from a probable overdose of heroin on December 30, 1970, in Las Vegas, that was Sonny's story, and he stuck to it.

The massive Foreman, the defending heavyweight champion, was flanked by aides including Archie Moore (second from right, in white hat) at the weigh-in in Kinshasa. (*AP Wirephoto*)

MUHAMMAD ALI vs. GEORGE FOREMAN

CHALLENGER   **CHAMPION**

HEAVYWEIGHT CHAMPIONSHIP

OCTOBER 30, 1974
KINSHASA, ZAIRE

ROUND 8

The seventies began with a mix of high hopes, kindling energy, and societal restlessness. Civil disobedience had rocked the land, segregation laws and other racial barriers came tumbling down, assassination was a frequently employed political solution, the FBI and CIA exceeded their authority and were restrained, and the nation woke up to the reality of a major global political mistake in Vietnam, the cost of which was dear in lives, dollars, and prestige. All over the country, morals collapsed in a decade of promiscuity made possible by the pill, which guaranteed protection against pregnancy; the growing prevalence of drugs; and the disintegration of the family unit.

THE FIGHT

If there is one color that comes to mind when I think back on the Muhammad Ali–George Foreman fight in Africa, it is black.

This was the first heavyweight championship fight that had a black champion (Foreman), black challenger (Ali), black promoter (Don King), black referee (Zack Clayton), and all-black host country, Zaire.

Black awareness had begun to make its presence felt in the seventies. For the first time since slavery, African-Americans took overt pride in their blackness. In doing so they rejected the insidious message, communicated through advertising and the media, that blacks should strive to be more "white" and less "black." As Ali would say with a twinkle in his eye, "Even the soap we use is Dove, a white bird; you don't see no 'Crow,' a black soap, do you?"

THE INCOMPARABLE ALI

For perspective on Ali and his place in history, I turn to his biographer Thomas Hauser.

Says Tom, "You really have to look at Muhammad Ali as bookends for the 1960s. To my way of thinking, the sixties began in an incredible three-month period that started with John Kennedy's assassination in late November of 1963. In January 1964 the Beatles come over to the United States and appear on the *Ed Sullivan Show*. In February 1964 Muhammad Ali knocks out Sonny Liston and becomes heavyweight champion of the world.

"In those three months you had a complete change in the social, political, and even the economic climate of this country. Then you fast-forward to the summer of 1974, 10 years later, when within the span of a couple of months Richard Nixon resigns, ending Watergate and the his presidency, and then Muhammad Ali dethrones George Foreman to capture the heavyweight championship of the world. Those two events, Nixon's resignation and Ali's ascension once again to the throne, really vindicated everything that the people who had fought so hard in the 1960s believed in."

Ali was presented to the world as a fresh-faced, sassy, charming man-child, winning a boxing gold medal at the Rome Olympics in 1960 and causing the American TV audience to sit up and take notice. His name was Cassius Marcellus Clay, and the press took to calling him the Louisville Lip. He was big, beautiful, and an irrepressible imp. He was lovable.

Ali's boxing feats are well-documented, but his claim to world fame derived from his uncommon strength of character. He became a Muslim minister. He prayed, he preached, he announced his conviction that the Vietnam War was wrong, and he refused to be drafted. Boxing's chieftains withdrew his title and forced him into a hard exile for three and a half years, preventing him from pursuing his livelihood. He was a rudderless ship in hostile seas.

Once again proving that he thrived on challenges, on going out on a limb then sawing it off, Ali hit the lecture circuit. With his phenomenal sense of timing and his inherent good luck, his exile coincided with the disillusionment of the vast white American middle class, many of whose kids were in revolt at their colleges. Ali had stumbled into a fertile field of empathy and likemindedness. The kids loved the big, handsome boxer with the million-dollar smile and the ability to turn anything into a laugh. He gained a broad base of support that would serve him well for the rest of his life.

After his enforced layoff, Ali returned to the ring in 1970 and promptly knocked out Jerry Quarry and then Oscar Bonavena. He lost a decision in a March 1971 title bout to Joe Frazier, the defending heavyweight champ, but seemed to grow in defeat. Ali then launched an intensive campaign to regain his title. The trail led to George Foreman—who had won the heavyweight crown with a second-round KO of Frazier in January 1973—and the memorable "Rumble in the Jungle."

GEORGE FOREMAN

George Foreman was a brooding, sullen character whose boxing ideal was Sonny Liston. Like Liston, Foreman was considered invincible. Like Liston, Foreman was so intimidating that opponents were often effectively "knocked out" before the opening bell. Like Liston, Foreman believed in his invincibility, believed that anyone who stood still in front of him would be bludgeoned into unconsciousness. Like Liston, Foreman believed there wasn't a man on Earth who could hurt, much less beat, him in the ring.

Outside the ring Foreman adopted Liston's scowling persona. Newsmen found him distant and, at times, threatening. The public was put off. Liston and Foreman were not popular men. Few kids aspired to be like George Foreman when he was the heavyweight champion.

Foreman's grim visage provided the promoters and publicity flacks with half of what they needed to make attractive matches: a villain, or, in wrestling parlance, a black hat.

DON KING

Don King's road to the "Rumble in the Jungle" was a thing of fiction, a Dickensian progression from petty street crime, murder, and incarceration to self-education and a series of serendipitous, fortunate turns that, if they were not true, would be hard to believe. Most big fortunes are made by stumbling into an opportunity and knowing how to take advantage of it. Timing, that indispensable element, has always been Don King's forte.

King had prospered as a Cleveland numbers dealer. He was amassing a decent bankroll when he had a "mathematical" dispute with an associate that escalated beyond words and into violence. King is a heavyset, 6'4" hulk of a man, and his temper is legendary. On this occasion he lost that temper, smote the man, and rendered him unconscious. Somewhere between the time when his fist struck the man and after the victim's head had hit a curbstone, life ebbed from the benighted fellow's body.

Don King was imprisoned for manslaughter. True to his nature, he used his time behind bars to improve himself. He read all of the *Harvard Classics* and Shakespeare and kept a *Webster's Dictionary* handy, and at the time of his parole he was a self-taught scholar with a penchant for flowery phrases. He came out of the joint a lot smarter than he went in. Always in a hurry, King wasted no time after his release. He had a plan to keep his eyes open for business opportunities that would make use of his talents and brains.

His timing was impeccable as usual. He fell in with the singer Lloyd Price, who requested Ali's assistance with a King-promoted charity boxing exhibition to benefit Forest City Hospital in Cleveland. Through this endeavor King was introduced to Don Elbaum, a well-known boxing promoter. They settled on the idea of presenting some exhibition boxing matches to raise the needed funds. Having thus gotten his foot in the door, Don King had assured his future in boxing. He had found his El Dorado.

King's exhibition bouts were a success, raising a reported $86,000. Today, Don Elbaum smiles wearily when he looks back on his venture with King. "Someone at the hospital told me they netted about $1,500," he says. The two Dons' relationship continued, with Elbaum, a generous guy, turning over to King a 50-percent share of heavyweight contender Earnie Shavers. After a few months, King's share of Shavers had increased to 100 percent. This was a Don King story that would be repeated over and over for many years. It was probably retold around the time of the 1974 Ali-Foreman fight in Zaire, when once again Don King was ready when opportunity knocked.

ZAIRE AND MOBUTU

When the Belgians left the Belgian Congo, they took everything European that they had brought there that wasn't bolted down. They even took the country's name, whereupon *Belgian Congo* became *Zaire* and *Leopoldville* was transformed into *Kinshasa*.

The problem faced by the new nation's president, Mobutu Sese Seko, who took office in 1965, was the seeming disappearance of Zaire from the world. Perhaps the new name needed some time to sink in, but for a while the nation's whereabouts confused many people. In Washington, D.C., a minister tried to mail a package to Zaire, but the postal clerk said he had never heard of the place. Asked to guess where it might be, the clerk answered, "An island in the Sea of Japan?"

Into this geographical void stepped Don King, bearing a hot contract signed by Ali and Foreman that would pay them $5 million each. And, King said gleefully, he was planning on this event's being a black "awakening." Along with the big fight, he would produce a huge jazz concert that would show his African brethren how far their American counterparts had come. Oh, it would be a joyous feast, and when Don King and Company were through, he promised, Zaire would be on the tip of everyone's tongue. Never again would anyone ask, "Zaire? Where is that?"

This was one promise that Don King would keep.

THE PREFIGHT HOOPLA

"Alice in Wonderland" was reborn in Kinshasha that fall. Mobutu wanted to look good for the visiting horde of tourists and media people. He repainted downtown Kinshasha. With no taxis to speak of, he ordered a fleet of cabs—very expensive Mercedes cars, as it turned out, because someone had somehow forgotten to check the price tag before delivery. It had been suggested that German cars should be purchased. The idea was Volkswagens, but Mobutu's minister heard "Mercedes."

Foreman grabbed the penthouse suite of Kinshasa's Hilton, leaving Ali stationed 20 miles from town, at Nsele, the presidential summer retreat. Foreman, suspicious, secretive, hostile, and paranoid, brought three huge police dogs to keep him company. Zairians, who had only recently been pursued by the Belgians' police dogs, did not appreciate his insensitive choice of companions.

Ali took to Africa like a grassroots politician, and Zaire readily fell in love with him. It was a quick, easy courtship, and in no time crowds were attending our training sessions, with drums booming and the people chanting "Ali, *boomaye*!" which meant "Ali, kill him!"

Ali led chorus after chorus, smiling broadly.

Bundini Brown got the bellboys at the Hilton to pass the word to Foreman that his food was being poisoned. Foreman bit like Charlie the Tuna. He began sending to America for all his food and water.

Meanwhile, the irrepressible Don King kept receiving slamming body blows. Money was always the problem. King did not promote this fight alone; Video Techniques, a British corporation, fronted most of the cash and the Zaire government put up the balance. But money was always tight.

The gigantic sum paid the fighters was a record at the time. To put it in perspective, Ali's purse of $5.45 million was more than Joe Louis ($4.6 million), Jack Dempsey ($3.5 million), or Rocky Marciano ($3 million) grossed in their entire careers.

Events quickly spiraled out of control. Posters bearing the slogan "From the Slave Ship to the Championship" proved insulting to Zairians, whose response was on the order of, "Hey, man, we're the ones that sold you away from here as slaves." It was an argument that was hard to rebut. King was forced to withdraw the posters and absorb the financial loss.

The fighters and President Mobutu presided over the opening of the 20th of May Stadium. (*AP Photo/Horst*)

The jazz concert was an unmitigated disaster. It was scheduled to start around midnight. Zairians, however, go to bed early in order to go to work early the next day. A concert featuring an unfamiliar kind of music would not keep them up past their bedtime. The concert died. A huge hole opened in the fight's budget, sending King and Lloyd Price on a mission to Liberia to seek a loan. This was very risky, for Mobutu was a man of immense ego. Liberia was a much-detested neighbor of Zaire, and Mobutu did not want to hear that King had been obliged to go begging for money from Liberia. For a while the situation was touch and go in terms of how safe the visiting Americans considered themselves. Mobutu was a man who frequently settled disputes and insults with a firing squad!

An acute problem surrounding tickets to the fight had developed. The fight was to be held at an old football stadium. The arena had concrete steps, like an old Roman coliseum, but no chairs or aisles and no floor plan. It was impossible to order tickets without this vital information, i.e., where one's seats would be located. "Print the tickets. We will adapt the stadium to the tickets," said one of Mobutu's government ministers.

The printed tickets arrived on a Tuesday, and everything seemed rosy until someone noticed that a *u* in President Mobutu's name had been replaced with an *o* on the tickets. The mistake cost the ticket man his life. Mobutu took things seriously; the price for screwing up was death. I hate to think of how many times Zairian officials considered administering some local justice to Don King for his continual foul-ups. At one point, the government allowed the jazz musicians to leave the country, but seized their instruments to guarantee payment of their room-service tab, which had amounted to $150,000 for the weekend!

Then, when everything seemed to be going wrong at the same time, Don King called upon his good-luck mojo. It was as if Ali's lifelong good fortune had rubbed off on King, who was no stranger to either good or bad luck.

George Foreman was hit with an elbow by his sparring partner. The resultant cut would postpone the fight for six weeks.

This turn of events was like the second Liston-Ali meeting, but in reverse. Ali was now in the role of the aging gladiator, with Foreman cast as the precocious kid. But Ali's luck would prevail again, as usual. He wouldn't meet the fate that Liston had suffered at his hands in Maine.

With six weeks to kill, Ali stretched out and relaxed, then embarked on an intensive training program designed to acclimate him to the African heat and humidity. Foreman dozed in air-conditioned comfort. Ali would be ready for the humid Zairian night when superior fitness would win the title. In retrospect, Foreman's laid-back training regimen left him no chance at crunch time.

Ali was not only fit, but beloved, wrapped up in an amazing groundswell of support from the people of Zaire. Ali was everywhere. On every street corner, it seemed, there he was, being seen, touched, kissed, and hugged by adoring followers, who adopted him as one of their own. Ali turned into an African. He had found his roots. These people loved him and would will him to win.

EARLY RUMBLINGS

Kinshasha was packed with media. The reporters, who often could be found crowded around the bar at the Hilton, shared a single, horrifying thought: how can we get our story out of here and on to our papers or stations back home? The local officials were cordial and effusive in their reassurances that all would be "no problem," a phrase that struck terror in media hearts. Few people believed that there would be no problem. And what would be the point of witnessing a great fight and having no way to get the story out to the rest of the world?

As the doctor in charge of Ali, I had a couple of problems when we arose at Nsele at two in the morning on the day of the fight, which would take place two hours later.

The main problem was the matter of numbing Ali's hands. C. B. Adkins, one of Herbert Muhammad's inner circle of advisers and one of the least accomplished members of this Ali Circus, had just expressed serious doubts about whether this should or would done. Adkins's claim to fame was that he had married two black singing stars, Della Reese and Sarah Vaughan. However admirable that feat was, it did not in any way qualify him as a medical specialist in hand injuries. It was C.B.'s quaint belief that numbing Ali's knuckles could in some way diminish the speed and accuracy of his punches. Considering that I had been numbing Ali's hands for several years, it seemed a tad late to bring up this possible drawback. I could not imagine why anyone even listened to Adkins's theory. Ali wanted the numbing done, I felt it had to be done, and our track record proved that it worked very well. What should C. B. have to do with anything? Still, the argument raged until it was almost time to leave for the stadium, at which point Ali and I went into the bathroom and numbed his hands while Bundini guarded the door.

My other problem arose when I ran into Herbert Muhammad's personal physician in the hotel lobby. Herbert had a variety of illnesses, most stemming from his overweight condition, and had apparently decided to bring his doctor along in case anything happened to him in Zaire. Whatever the reason, the good doctor could not restrain himself from examining Ali and proclaiming that he had hypoglycemia. This is an impossible diagnosis to reach without doing lab work. It is also not a serious illness in any case.

It was with some amusement that I heard this physician announce his recommendation that on fight night, preferably right before entering the ring, Ali ingest a deep-dish peach cobbler with a pint of vanilla ice cream on top. Lana Shabazz, the cook for Ali's team, was ready to prepare this confection if so ordered. Even a first-year medical student is taught never to give sugar to someone with hypoglycemia. This forces the insulin to oversecrete, and the patient passes out. I was ready to eat the cobbler myself before I would let Ali go near it.

Such were the sensibilities afloat that day that I did not want to precipitate a crisis by denouncing the other doctor as incompetent. Instead, the order of the day was "make do, don't make waves." I assured the doctor that I would pour a pound of sugar into an orange juice bottle and feed it to the hypoglycemic Ali as the fight progressed, to "keep his gas tank filled" (in the words of the good doctor). That bottle is still in the jungle, lying in tall grass somewhere between Nsele and the football stadium.

Angelo Dundee had his own troubles to deal with on the day of the fight. Angelo, who is very cautious by nature, went to examine the ring with Bobby Goodman, the fight's publicity man. They found the newly constructed ring in appalling condition. The ring canvas was new but loose. They had to summon a crew to tighten it and tack it down. The ring ropes were another major problem. They sagged and drooped in the middle. Bobby and Angelo got hold of big screwdrivers and went to work on the turnbuckles in each corner. Despite expending plenty of effort, they could only do so much. The ropes were still loose and still sagged. Angelo made a mental note to tell Ali not to lean on the ropes, or he'd end up flying headfirst into the press section.

It is a source of continuous amusement to me to read that Angelo Dundee is considered the architect of Ali's famous rope-a-dope maneuver because he loosened the ropes that day. Angelo, at first bewildered by the erroneous reporting, now just smiles and shrugs.

"I thought we were in deep trouble because the heat in Zaire had stretched those hemp ropes," says Angelo. "I was afraid that Foreman would miss a shot, hit Ali with an elbow on the chest, and my guy would right go out of the ring; end of fight. I thought the kid would get hurt if that happened because it was a high ring, for TV purposes."

The dressing rooms were big and primitive. Our sizable entourage went inside Ali's and spread out. Norman Mailer later reported that there was an aura of fear and anxiety in the room. As I recall, the only writer in the room was Budd Schulberg, and the atmosphere was one of guarded confidence. After all, big nights were part of life in the Ali Circus, and we had all been in this position before. Ali loved the pressure. He was always "on" when the press and/or the odds were against him. For this fight he was an 8-to-1 underdog! Once again I had brought along a sack of money to bet, and once again I was shut out from the action. Who was there to bet with? When Ali heard about the 3–1 odds, he began smiling. "I'll shock and amaze 'em!" he boasted. "I'll shock the world!"

The night before the fight had unfolded strangely in George Foreman's penthouse hotel suite. First, Foreman, taking a page out of Liston's gangster handbook, had called Don King and informed him that he would not fight unless he was paid an additional $500,000 beyond the $5 million he was already getting. Foreman issued an ultimatum: If this money wasn't delivered, there would be no fight. The unflappable King responded with silky smoothness, producing a check that was drawn on a London bank and could be cashed in London on Monday, after the fight. George greedily grabbed the check, unaware that Don King was the master of the old give-and-go. It turned out that King had privately offered each fighter an incentive bonus for winning the bout. Of course only one of them would win and collect the bonus, and that would be Ali. George probably still has that check in his scrapbook.

More bizarre was Foreman's visit with Tshimpumpu Wa Tshimpumpu, who was the main government minister in charge of the fight. George greeted him in his quarters the night before the fight with a peculiar demand.

Foreman declared, "I want to fight Joe Bugner after I knock out Ali."

The minister, envisioning another windfall for his nation and relishing how much that would please Mobutu, was happy to oblige. "Certainly. That can be arranged. I will be glad to get in touch with Mr. Bugner," he said.

"I mean fight him after Ali," said George.

"Certainly. When?" replied the minister.

"Now. Tomorrow night. After Ali."

"You mean you think you'll knock out Ali, then you want to fight Bugner right away? The same night?"

"Yes. I want this done."

This of course was absurdly impossible. The notion of getting in touch with Bugner, signing him, having him travel to Africa, and so on, all within the next 24 hours, left Tshimpumpu questioning George's sanity. Foreman had indeed been acting strange, the minister mused, and his demands were usually outlandish.

Tshimpumpu raced to N'sele to tell Ali of his peculiar visit with Foreman. Ali greeted the news with a broad smile.

"Now I know I got 'the Mummy.' He thinks he's going to knock me out in three rounds? He's mine now!"

Foreman was like Liston in more ways than he knew!

THE FIGHT

The Rumble in the Jungle took place in the early hours of an African morning with storm clouds overhead portending rain and another possible cancellation. The 20 of May Stadium, as it was named, was packed with 60,000 fans on the 30 of October, 1974. The setting was exotic, to say the least. African dancers performed in tribal regalia, the Zairian fans chanted "Ali, boomaye," and Foreman had one of his sparring partners circulating in the stadium with a bullhorn, chanting, "Oh yeah, oh yeah, Ali in three!" over and over.

The ring was small. The referee, Zack Clayton, said that it measured a standard 18 feet square, but the ropes fit a 24-foot ring; hence the sagging strands.

The press section was packed with big-name writers and sportscasters. The popular television interviewer David Frost was doing blow-by-blow commentary for a network while Jim Brown, the Hall of Fame NFL fullback, provided the expert commentary. Neither man had ever covered a fight before; welcome to the craziness of Zaire. The only one around with any boxing expertise was the seasoned broadcaster "Colonel" Bob Sheridan, whose accurate, insightful commentary can be heard today on the TV tape of the fight.

One of my close friends, Jerry Lisker of the *New York Post*, had arranged and paid dearly for a private telephone feed to New York, courtesy of a high-ranking Zairian official. Lisker now held an earphone to his head and a microphone to his mouth. "Okay?" he asked. "Okay" came the clear answer through the headset. Lisker was ready. He would have a scoop: a blow-by-blow story as it happened, in "real time."

In the ring, Clayton motioned to the timekeeper. At the bell Ali ran over and hit Foreman with a hard right to the head, just as he had said he would. "I want him to feel my punch so he knows he's in for a tough night," had been Ali's words.

The beginning of this fight would resemble Ali's first bout with Liston, as a confident Foreman stalked Ali just as Sonny had in the early going. Ali bounced on fresh legs, bipping and bopping with his flicking, Willie Pastrano–style jab. Foreman's punches suited Ali's nickname for his opponent, the Mummy—sweeping, wide, ponderous. Occasionally, they landed on Ali's trim body, but if they had any effect he didn't show it. Ali continued to dance. Foreman's face stayed unexpressive; masklike, mummified. Like Liston, Foreman was used to fighting an opponent who ran away from him. They

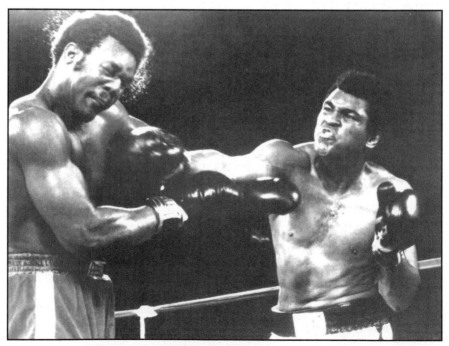

Ali played rope-a-dope in the early rounds, then hammered Foreman with hard rights. (*Hank Kaplan Archives*)

would for a while, but eventually they would slow down and find themselves pinned against the ropes, whereupon George would unleash his siege guns and batter the foe into unconsciousness.

Ali returned to his corner as the bell sounded, ending Round 1. Perspiration flowed in rivulets down his handsome face. "He hits hard, but not so hard I can't take it. Liston hit harder," he said, adding, "It's hot out there. It's muggy. Hard to breathe."

We were all busy with our tasks. Only Angelo spoke, and he had nothing to say except, "Keep on doing what you're doing. Stay off the ropes. Don't let him catch you on the ropes!"

Naturally, as was so often the case, Ali did just the opposite of what Angelo had instructed.

No one can possibly guess what goes through Ali's mind; not even Norman Mailer, who writes as if he had a room reserved in the fighter's cranium. Ali himself can't tell you where his inspiration comes from, any more than Picasso could identify the origin of *Guernica* or Duke Ellington the source of *Mood Indigo*. I believe that Muhammad Ali is a boxing genius. He doesn't intellectualize, thinking things through and drawing conclusions. Ali just does. Boxing is all reflex. No one had Ali's reflexes, not even the great Sugar Ray Robinson.

Something in Ali's brain told him to go to the ropes and see how Foreman reacted. A daring gamble? More like a suicidal urge, with George Foreman at large in the vicinity. When Foreman saw Ali fall against the ropes, his feet spread apart and his back resting on the top strand, which sagged dangerously, he licked his lips.

George announced the opening of his attack with two sweeping hooks. Ali took both hooks, a right and a left, on his arms. George didn't take notice that he had failed to hit his target, Ali's ribs. Now he switched targets, launching a fearsome left hook at Ali's head. This punch also missed its mark, glancing off Ali's glove.

In the corner we were having the equivalent of an African nervous breakdown. The exact thing that we had dreaded was happening. All the months of training to avoid getting caught on the ropes was going out the window.

"Get off the ropes!" Angelo shouted. He was up on the top step, his face strained, the veins in his neck distended, terror in his voice. "Get outta there, Ali!"

Behind him the rest of the corner crew—Bundini, Walter "Bloods" Youngblood, Luis Sarria, and I—screamed the same thing. Even the old veteran Sarria, Ali's Spanish-speaking Cuban masseuse, yelled in English, "Off the ropes!"

Ali stayed on the ropes till the end of the round. What we, in our panic, had failed to notice was a miniature preview of what was to come—what Ali's genius had concocted for George Foreman.

What we had not seen was a fleeting blur of an event. As Foreman had withdrawn to the perimeter, Ali had hit him with a lightning-fast combination: left jab, hard right cross, left hook. George blinked. He looked surprised. Where had that come from? He would find out that there was more of the same in store for him.

Angelo started to yell as soon as Ali sat down. Ali held up his glove, like a king calling for silence.

"Shut up. I know what I'm doing."

We all worked hard, massaging his arms and legs, dousing him with cooling water, applying ice bags to his head, neck, and face. Ali appeared relaxed. Before the bell rang, he said to no one in particular, "He don't hit so hard."

The third and fourth rounds were awful for us to watch. I felt that this great kid, our hero, was going to be hurt, really hurt. I reviewed in my mind the choices of where to take him in the event of a head injury. There were no facilities whatsoever in Zaire. Maybe we could get a jet to Madrid, hours away, if all went well. I started to pray.

Mills Lane, viewing the tape of the fight at this juncture, observes, "You can see Foreman's punches are just lumbering. He is just kind of pushing them. Ali is a smart guy. He's covering up, he's pushing his head down a little bit, and every now and again he throws something. But Foreman has got nothing left. Nothing at all."

Meanwhile, above me in the ring, Ali added another element to his act: dialogue. He began to talk to Foreman. "Oooh, George, that left hook stung me. Don't throw that no more." Even more surprising, Foreman was listening to him.

"Ali talks to Foreman," says Tom Hauser, following the action on tape. "It's important for people to remember that when Ali went to the ropes, he didn't just lie there, taking punches. He blocked a lot of the punches with his forearms, leaned back from others, and most important, he threw punches off the ropes. He won three of the first four rounds. In the fifth round he started to tire, but of course he came back later on."

Foreman, speaking on TV years later, admitted that Ali had him thinking. Questions raced through George's mind: Is he kidding? Is this a trap? Does he want to bait me into throwing another left hook so he can counter it? Should I fake the left and throw the right? What is he thinking?

Ali indeed had Foreman thinking, which was right where he wanted him. In the thinking department, Foreman was a Model T to Ali's Maserati.

As I said earlier, boxing is all reflex; very, very little thinking is involved. While Foreman was taking a multiple-choice test in his brain, Ali was rattling hard combinations off his head. And make no mistake, Ali can punch—very hard. Foreman had never before been rattled like this.

It was hot. Oh, Lord, was it hot and muggy. The conditions were nearly intolerable in and around the ring.

Foreman now began to pay the price for having chosen to relax in the air-conditioned splendor of the Hilton penthouse while Ali acclimated himself to the African heat. Foreman sagged visibly. His punches lost their steam. He was pushing "pillow" punches, not zinging blasters. His eyes betrayed confusion and weariness. He had Ali on the ropes, but he couldn't hit him cleanly. Even when he did, the shots did not seem to faze Ali.

Ali always made the best of any bad breaks that came his way. So the ropes sagged? Ali found that he could lean back so far on them that Foreman couldn't reach him with a fishing pole.

Boxing fans tend to forget that Ali is 6-foot-3 and supple. You'd need to catch a cab to get to him when his rangy frame reclined back on loose rope strands. But we didn't appreciate this in his corner at the time; all we noticed was Foreman punching while Ali lay back on those ropes, and we were concerned.

As the fourth round ended, we breathed a slight sigh of relief when Ali came back to the corner smiling.

"I've got him now," he told us. "I'll knock him out when I want to!"

"Well, please do it," implored Dundee. Angelo had been with this kid since the beginning. He knew Ali better than anyone did. Sometimes I felt that Angelo knew Ali better than he knew himself. They were a great team.

"Please, baby, knock this guy out!" Angelo begged.

"Not yet. He's had his turn. Now comes my time to play." To our consternation, Ali was having fun! Things could go wrong. Foreman could land a lucky punch. But, as always, Ali was going to do what he wanted to do, and he knew what he had to do.

Round 5 was a different kind of dance. Ali took the lead, with George stumbling after his fleet foe. Ali wasn't exactly dancing, but he was moving with fluid grace, popping his jab in Foreman's swelling face and then nailing him with cruel, hard, straight right hands. A disbelieving Foreman, whose programmed style was always to move forward and annihilate the enemy, lumbered toward Ali. Rounds 5, 6, and 7 were boxing lessons taught by Ali. He was looking good. From time to time, when he decided he needed a rest, he reverted to rope-a-dope. Foreman failed to grasp the fact that by continuing to hurl punches at the reclining Ali, he was expending precious strength and energy in the sweltering heat.

At one point in the seventh round, Ali wrestled an exhausted Foreman into a clinch in his own corner, so that Foreman leaned back against the ropes with Ali facing George's corner. Working in that corner was Ali's onetime mentor, Archie Moore, the former light-heavyweight champion, who was now 70 years old. Moore grasped the ropes, yelling instructions to Foreman. He was a desperate cornerman at that instant, trying as hard as he could to help his endangered fighter. Ali momentarily caught Moore's eye, shook his head, and said in a clear voice, "Be quiet, old man. It's all over."

Ali came back to a much more relaxed corner at the end of Round 7.

"I gotta get him this round. I'm starting to get very tired," he announced.

"Well, do it, champ. Enough of this. Knock the chump out!" Angelo exhorted. Dundee was yelling, begging, encouraging; doing whatever it might take to motivate Ali to finish the job, preferably with a clean knockout.

As the eighth round got under way, Ali played Foreman as Manolete would play a prize Miura bull. George was dazed, tired, and confused. He seemed to want nothing more than a safe place to land. We held our breath. What was Ali waiting for?

Archie Moore was frustrated that his sage ring advice was not being heeded. Later he would say, "I told him that he must not let Ali pull his head down. The way to avoid this was to hit him with both hands to the body when Ali held."

The main man in Foreman's corner was Dick Sadler, a savvy cornerman but no Archie Moore when it came to experience and ring wisdom. Moore, "the Old Mongoose," had fought for 30 years and would be inducted into the International Boxing Hall of Fame.

"Let him fight his own fight," shouted Sadler angrily at Moore. "George knows what's best for George." Sadly, George didn't.

With 20 seconds to go in the round and Foreman flailing around the ring on unsteady legs, Ali pressed the Destruct button. He unleashed a beautiful series of four hard, left-right combinations, catching Foreman flush on the jaw. Oh, Ali was a sharpshooter. His aim was unerring.

Foreman's jaw went slack. His eyes turned glassy and blank. Jackknifing, his massive body sank to the canvas in perfect Esther Williams form. Referee Zack Clayton began the count without hesitation. As Clayton reached nine, George struggled up, but he was out on his feet and Clayton signaled that it was all over. An instant later the bell rang. Clayton had never reached 10 in his count. Would the bell have saved Foreman if he had had another second or two, and then, after the bell sounded, time between rounds to clear his head in his corner?

Says Mills Lane, "If Foreman gets up by nine and everything is off the deck except the soles of his shoes, he's entitled to go back to the corner (after the bell) and see if he can get it together. It might not have made the difference, but that is not the issue. The question is, Was the officiating technically correct? It was not. When a fighter goes down, he's entitled to 10 counts. Rarely is a 10-count equal to 10 seconds. It might be 11, it might be nine, it might be 12. But when the fighter who is down looks up from the deck and sees the ref counting "four, five, six," he's entitled to believe that the next count is going to be seven; and after that, eight and nine; and that if he gets up by eight or nine, he's up, no matter how long that count actually took."

So, could George Foreman have been saved by the bell? Maybe. But the beating that was undoubtedly in store for him could have caused serious harm. Moreover, no one from his corner was arguing. The Rumble in the Jungle was over. Ali had put his signature on his masterpiece.

In the ringside crowd I picked out the strained face of Jerry Lisker, the *New York Post* sportswriter, who had been dictating his fevered description of the action to a man on the other side of the ring, whose hands were clasped over the earphones he was wearing. Lisker was finished now. He had dictated a first-rate story, and he was sure that he had beaten his cohorts to the punch, scooped them. Lisker looked again at his partner across the ring, whose job was to relay Lisker's words over a secure line to the *Post* newsroom in New York. The man was smiling broadly, giving Lisker a thumbs-up. Lisker began to get a sinking feeling in the pit of his stomach.

"Okay?" asked Lisker feebly, hoping his fears were unfounded.

"Okay," replied the man. "Transmit whenever you're ready, Mr. Lisker."

And then the African skies opened and we were drenched by the downpour. The gods who look after Ali and confer inhuman luck on him had waited until the eighth round, until his work was finished, before releasing this deluge that soaked the stadium crowd.

Back from exile, Muhammad Ali had reclaimed his heavyweight championship. Once more, he had defied the odds. Once more, he had, in his words, "shocked and amazed the world!"

AFTERMATH

The Rumble in the Jungle and the surrounding adventure in Zaire had different effects on different people.

George Foreman certainly didn't get to fight Joe Bugner, and he didn't get that extra $500,000. As the winner, Ali did get the additional half-million. He earned $5,450,000 that night, boxing's biggest paycheck to date. Ali thus inaugurated the era of the Big Purse.

Don King established himself as a force in boxing, and for a while he kept Ali in his stable. He had pioneered holding a fight in a foreign country. He had introduced the $5 million purse. And he had become what he had set out to be: boxing's first, biggest, and best black promoter. In time the qualifying word *black* was dropped from the phrase, because King was simply the biggest promoter of any color in boxing history.

My own lasting impression of Zaire came on the 40-mile ride back to Nsele after the fight. We were in a convoy of limos and buses. The rain was heavy, and as we drove through it I became aware of phantasmal figures appearing from the depths of the thick jungle. This strange sight was repeated all the way back to training camp. The figures were people. The natives had brought their children to the side of the road to watch the great Muhammad Ali pass by. They held palm fronds, pieces of corrugated tin, or colored slabs of plastic over the children's heads to protect them from the rain. It reminded me of the masses of Americans who lined the railroad tracks to glimpse the great war president Franklin D.

Roosevelt's funeral train as it passed by. They couldn't see Roosevelt, of course; they just wanted to pay tribute with their presence. So it was all the way along this journey back to Nsele. The people were there to pay silent tribute to the new king, Muhammad Ali.

I watched this unfold while sitting with the great boxing aficionado-writer Budd Schulberg, and we were both struck silent by the scene we beheld. Finally, I said, "Now Ali belongs to the world."

And so he did.

Meanwhile, George Foreman was in bad shape, suffering from exhaustion and dehydration. He would need plenty of time to recover. After several more fights, many of them exhibitions, Foreman retired for a decade or so, which he spent preaching at a small church in the Houston ghetto. Coincidentally or not, when his ministerial calling and a zero bank balance intersected, Foreman returned to fighting, won a championship, became a portly folk hero, made roughly a zillion dollars, and contentedly ate about 80 million hamburgers.

It remains for Ali's biographer Thomas Hauser to describe the historical significance of the Rumble in the Jungle, whose eighth round ranks as one of the most important of the 20th century.

"Muhammad Ali beating George Foreman was the classic sports fairy tale," says Tom. "It's the story of the handsome prince who, unfairly deprived of his crown, comes back and regains the throne.

"This was an enormously important fight for Ali. When all is said and done, this fight meant more to Muhammad than any other fight in his career. It was important that it was in Africa because you had two black fighters and you had Don King as a very visible presence. This was an African nation, and Ali used that reality to fuel himself.

"Let me encapsulate this African experience. It was, to my way of thinking, a black awakening, a reassurance to the black race that they were beautiful, they were good, they were something to aspire to be. This fight proved to Americans that blacks could participate in the management part of an event. Don King proved he could be an international promoter who took care of everything, including satellite television. When it was over, we ended up with the next era in boxing."

Frazier and Ali fought three times, culminating in the historic 1975 Thrilla in Manila. (*George Kalinsky*)

FIGHT OF THE CENTURY

MUHAMMAD ALI vs. JOE FRAZIER

CHAMPION   **CHALLENGER**

HEAVYWEIGHT CHAMPIONSHIP

MANILA, PHILIPPINES
OCTOBER 1, 1975

ROUND 14

In the mid-1970s the United States was recovering slowly from the social upheavals of the sixties. Political protests shook the public into an awareness that the nation's involvement in Vietnam had been badly misguided. The war finally ended with the withdrawal of U.S. embassy personnel in 1975. Assassination attempts on prominent figures continued to be an unsettling fact of American life, as President Ford survived two failed attempts on his life. The public's spirit was leavened in 1975, however, by baseball's World Series, as the Cincinnati Reds edged the Boston Red Sox four games to three in one of history's most exciting Fall Classics.

Meanwhile, the world's population passed 4 billion. In a historic first, the Soviets' Soyuz craft linked in space with the Americans' Apollo 18, inaugurating an era of cooperation in space by the two superpowers.

In boxing, Muhammad Ali continued to take his Ali Circus to various foreign countries. In 1975 the traveling spectacle set sail for the Philippines and what was expected to be an easy fight with an old adversary, Joe Frazier.

It would turn out to be anything but that.

THE BACKGROUND

The greatest fight of the century was not considered much of a fight when it was made. It seemed like an "oh, by the way" kind of promotion by Don King; an afterthought.

King had found yet another country badly in need of a divertissement. He would provide it, in the form of a sporting event that would capture the world's interest while distracting the Filipino people's attention from the rebels in the country's mountains, the nation's sagging economy, and the humid heat of October. President Ferdinand Marcos would be grateful for the opportunity to host a happening featuring the charismatic world heavyweight champion, Muhammad Ali. For his part Ali was eager to get out of his own country. He sought escape for the oldest of reasons: love. Ali needed to escape the bonds of his marriage.

In Africa the previous year Ali had met a gorgeous girl, Veronica Porche, and had fallen head over heels in love. The relationship grew increasingly serious in the ensuing months. Belinda, Ali's long-suffering wife and the mother of his children, seemed powerless to stop the affair. Ali was a man in lust.

A fight in the Philippines would allow Ali to be alone with Veronica for at least six weeks. Belinda would be left behind to tend to the children. This was too good to pass up. Ali enthusiastically signed the contract.

Joe Frazier's stock had fallen to a low point since beating Ali in their first fight, in 1971. In 1973 Frazier had entered the ring with George Foreman, who treated Smokin' Joe as his personal yo-yo, bouncing him off the canvas until he knocked him out in the second round. In a return match with Ali in Madison Square Garden in 1974, Joe had been beaten handily in losing a 12-round decision. Joe Frazier was on the skids.

Muhammad Ali is a loving man. He cannot hold a grudge. He always treats former opponents with great warmth and affection, and he had an especially soft spot in his heart for Joe Frazier. His first encounter with Frazier had been one of the greatest fights in his career, even though he had lost the 15-round decision in a superb contest of wills. Now Ali, the victor in the '74 rematch, felt sorry for Frazier. He wanted to give him a going-away present. Frazier would come to the Philippines, take his beating, and go home with a truck load of retirement money. Ali and his people agreed it would be a decent thing to do for the man who had provided Ali such invaluable, high-profile exposure. In his singular way, Ali loved Frazier. Frazier forced him to fight at the top of his form.

Says Angelo Dundee, "Joe Frazier wasn't a safe opponent for anybody. Frazier on any given night could lick any given fighter because he was—he was for real. The only problem he had was that Muhammad Ali was around, and Muhammad Ali could always beat Joe Frazier."

In Frazier's corner there was no love lost for the opponent who proclaimed himself the Greatest. Joe Frazier truly despised Ali. Joe was a tough man from the mean streets of Philadelphia. His road to the top had been hard; his fights typically were brutal slugging matches. However tough, Frazier was an honorable man, a noble warrior who loved his family. Physically, he was the antithesis of Ali: short (a shade under six feet), heavily muscled, and frequently scowling. As such, he was the perfect foil for Ali, who loved to tease his opponents, often focusing his barbs on an aspect of their appearance. Frazier had a deep, glowing pride in who he was and what he had become. He saw nothing funny about his looks, but Ali did. Ali called him "the Gorilla."

For Joe, this fight wasn't about money. He took what was offered; there wasn't even a meaningful negotiation. Ali was guaranteed $4 million against 43 percent of all fight-generated income. Frazier would end up with half of Ali's eventual take of $6 million.

Frazier requested accommodations for 17 people in Manila. Ali said he needed plane tickets and lodging for 50, and by the time his full entourage had arrived in the Philippines, it numbered considerably more than 50. You see, Joe Frazier was in Manila on business. Muhammad Ali was there on holiday.

The Ali Circus, which had seriously begun to gather steam in Zaire, reached its zenith—or nadir, depending on your perspective— in Manila. The increasingly bloated size of the Circus was not the result of Ali's generosity, although that was legendary. What made these sideshows possible was the governments of the countries hosting the fights, which provided airline tickets and hotel accommodations at no cost. At that price Ali invited the world, and his world came to consist of an eclectic group of ex-fighters, boxing managers, agents, pimps and their whores, movie stars between pictures, beauty queens, rock stars, writers, painters, facilitators, tourist guides, politicians, gangsters, procurers, drug dealers, and garden-variety con men.

All we lacked was a priest, but we had an entire college of cardinals in the form of the Muslim hierarchy led by Herbert Muhammad, who was Ali's manager and the son of the Right Honorable Elijah Muhammad. We didn't lack for spiritual help.

The presence of such a glut of parasites might be expected to have an adverse effect on a boxing champion who is preparing to defend his crown. In this case there were other deleterious distractions for the fighter: he was on a secret honeymoon, he seriously underestimated his challenger, and he viewed his visit to Manila as an all-expenses-paid, six-week vacation. Put these together and you have a formula for disaster.

As soon as Don King announced the fight, he labeled it the "Thrilla in Manila," which Ali impishly amended to the "Thrilla in Manila with the Gorilla." He even brought a toy gorilla doll to the press conference and gleefully punched it as cameras clicked.

Whenever Joe Frazier made the mistake of letting himself get caught seated beside Ali in a television studio or at a press conference, the results were painful to behold.

"I'm gonna . . . ," Frazier started to say in one interview.

"I'm going to . . . ," Ali enunciated clearly, correcting Joe as if he were a dumb ghetto kid. "Not 'I'm gonna.' Talk intelligent," Ali said, smiling patronizingly at Joe, who reacted badly; you could almost see smoke issuing from his ears. Doggedly, determined not to let Ali deflect his train of thought, Joe plowed on.

"I'm gonna go inta training . . ."

"Not *inta*," Ali interrupted. "*Into*. Say, how far did you go in school?"

"As far as you went," Frazier snarled.

"You don't look that way. Why do you say *dat-uh*?" As the crowd of photographers and writers began to laugh openly, Ali gathered momentum. "*Dat-uh*—what is that, Joe? What's *dat-uh*? The word is *that*, not *dat-uh*. Say *that*."

At this point it looked like Joe would explode and cold-cock Ali right there, but he was restrained before he could attack.

Knowing that he was well under Joe's skin, Ali pulled out the

Promoter Don King touted the fight—and himself—at a New York press conference. (*AP/Wide World Photos*)

little black-rubber gorilla doll and began to recite his doggerel
to a delighted audience:

"It will be a Killer
And a Chiller
And a Thriller
When I Get the Gorilla
In Manila."

Then he began to punch the gorilla doll— bip, bip, bip, bip;
five, six, seven times.

"All night long," Ali sang out, and from behind him Bundini
Brown echoed his sing-song refrain, "All night long!" Ali
punched the doll again for good measure, then added, "Come
on, Gorilla, this is a thrilla; come on, we in Manila."

Joe Frazier was hurt, bewildered, and angry. At the door of
his limousine, he faced the reporters' microphones. "He's talking now," said Joe, "but the time comin' when he gonna hear the
knock on the door, when it's time to come in the ring, and then
he's gonna remember what it's like to be in with me, how hard
and long that night's gonna be!"

Frazier had accepted this fight in a state of cold fury. He had
beaten Ali in the first fight, yet never got the glory he believed
that he deserved. Sure, some people complimented his victory
as workmanlike, but somehow the glory had accrued to Ali,
who had only recently returned to action following his exile.
People made excuses for him: he had come back too soon, he
wasn't ready yet for a championship bout. Moreover, some boxing scribes and other observers thought that Ali had won that
'71 encounter in New York, despite having been knocked down
by Frazier. Joe went into the hospital for six weeks after the
fight, they pointed out. As for the second fight, Joe blocked it
out of his mind as a bad night, an aberration.

Ali, meanwhile, was basking in the sunshine of overwhelm-
ing public adoration and enjoying the forbidden fruits of his
Asian tryst with Veronica. He escorted her openly around
Manila, enjoying the envious looks cast by other men. He made
his big mistake, however, when he took her to the Presidential

Palace to meet Marcos and his comely wife, Imelda.

Ali introduced the radiant Veronica as his wife.

"Your wife is quite beautiful," said Marcos, himself a connoisseur of fine ladies.

"Your wife ain't so bad herself," shot back Ali, his handsome face leering at Imelda, who smiled back.

A *Newsweek* article soon described the meeting to the world. Belinda exploded in all directions when she saw it. Her first act of vengeance was to board a plane to Manila. By the time she landed there, she knew that her marriage to Ali was over.

For Ali, training seemed to run a distant third among his priorities, behind public appearances throughout the Philippines and his torrid affair with Veronica. All eyes were on the champion and his extravagant activities. Even the rebels stopped fighting and filtered into Manila to watch the Ali Circus in action.

The stage was set. Ali, laughing and taunting "the Gorilla," anticipated an easy fight. Joe Frazier, dressed in workingman's denim and snorting fire, couldn't wait for the first round to arrive, freeing him to attack and destroy his nemesis, the only man on this planet to make fun of his looks and even demean his blackness. Frazier didn't just want to win and wrest Ali's title from him. He wanted to kill Ali.

The fight would be held at 10:30 a.m. at the Philippine Coliseum, in downtown Manila, It seemed pointless to announce an attendance figure, since by the time the fight started, Filipinos had oozed into every nook and cranny of the steaming arena. There were no longer aisles, just a wall-to-wall carpet of sweating people. The more athletic and daring spectators had even crawled out onto the rafters. The line of windows at the top of the arena was blocked by the uppermost edge of the throng.

There was no air conditioning. The high humidity in surrounding Manila and the temperature in the arena made breathing nearly impossible. Under the ring lights it was even hotter. Never before in my 40 years of boxing involvement had I experienced heat like this. I survived the corner work by wearing a towel that was soaked in cold water and filled with ice cubes on top of my head. Even this didn't help much.

The fighters were called to the middle of the ring by Carlos Padilla, a diminutive Filipino referee. My first thought was, "Oh God, how is that midget going to control these two giants?" It wasn't an idle thought.

Frazier stared hard at Ali. Smoke seemed to emanate from Smokin' Joe's nostrils, and he pawed the canvas with his foot. He looked like he wanted to hit Ali during the introductions. He was ready to go.

Ali looked serene, as if he were expecting a game of tennis. His mouth was still running, still joking at the expense of the Gorilla. His eyes twinkled. This, he thought, was going to be fun.

But it wouldn't be fun. It would be a battle nearly to the death, an epic struggle in three stages: stage one, which might be called Ali's Easy Time; stage two, Frazier's Turn; and stage three, The Shootout.

THE THREE-STAGE STRUGGLE

Ali came out on fresh legs at the opening bell, easily dodging Frazier's bull-like rushes. He blocked Joe's punches on his shoulders and gloves or slipped out of range, causing Frazier to swing wildly in the air. Ali was beautiful, and Joe . . . well, Joe was the Gorilla. Enough said. This was going to be easy.

In the second round Ali suddenly decided to fight flat-footed and go for the knockout—to shock and amaze the world. He rained blows on Joe, whose ability to take a punch had been questioned since Foreman had bounced him around like a basketball a year ago in Jamaica. Now Frazier kept coming, cannonball shots caroming off his iron jaw, and then he suddenly was staggered. Frazier was in trouble! Ali saw this and pursued him relentlessly. After Frazier had made it safely to the bell, Ali began to view him in a different light. This wasn't going to be easy after all. Joe banged his gloves together in his corner as he waited for Round 3 to begin.

The third round was more of the same. Ali would flick a powerful jab at Frazier, who seemed mesmerized by the punch. Then Ali would connect with a pile-driving right. Frazier's head would snap back, sweat flying, as his knees buckled. Twice more he seemed ready to fall, but he did not. Ali returned to the attack, confident that no man could take this punishment for long.

By the fourth round Ali's punches had lost their zing. He was tiring. The heat; the bright lights; the muggy, oxygen-deprived atmosphere; and the toughness of his opponent were wearing him down. It showed in small ways. Ali's customary composure lapsed at the end of the round when, with Frazier still on his feet, glowering like a wolf through his bloody mouthpiece, Ali snapped, "You dumb chump, you!"

"Around the fourth round, when Joe started cooking, I knew we were in for a long night," says Angelo Dundee.

Questions hung in the air. How much more could Frazier take? How much more did Ali have to give? His long days and nights of partying and lovemaking had suddenly become a factor. Frazier had trained to go 15 hard rounds if necessary. Ali hoped to be back at his hotel suite with Veronica by the end of Round 5. But here was Round 5, and Joe Frazier was still there in front of him and, worse, now advancing on him, windmilling damaging body punches.

While Ali continued to win the rounds on points, the momentum was slowly shifting. Now Ali backed into a corner and stayed there, permitting Frazier to pound his arms and body. It was the African rope-a-dope again, only this time his opponent, unlike the quickly exhausted Foreman, was ready to go the distance. Our corner yelled, "Quit playing!" Angelo, up on the top step, hoarsely yelling to be heard above the din, exhorted Ali, "Get out of the goddamn corner." But Ali stayed in a corner, on the ropes. Perhaps he couldn't get himself out of there.

Stage one ended around the close of Round 5, whereupon stage two, Frazier's Turn, began. Joe Frazier's fights had their own rhythm and style. Frazier often took a beating in the early rounds, but then his hard heart took over. Discouraged opponents caved in as Joe turned on his afterburners and launched his relentless, all-out attack.

Frazier's heart, his determination to win, surfaced during Round 5. His trademark evil left hook began beating a tattoo on Ali's ribs and kidneys. Frazier put his head on Ali's chest, pushed Ali back using his powerful thick legs, and let fly punches to Muhammad's body. Ali winced and tried to dance away from the mayhem, but Frazier's head seemed sewn to Ali's sternum. They embraced each other in a grotesque tango, Ali receiving steady punishment as the two fighters lurched across the ring. Suddenly, at the end of the fifth, Ali's legs were visibly turning to rubber. He knew he was getting into trouble, entering a zone he called "the dark room where you are searching for the light switch."

"Lord, that man can punch," gasped Ali as he joined us in the corner. We all looked at one another. He'd never said anything like that to us—not while fighting Sonny Liston, not while battling George Foreman, and not while tussling with Frazier in their two previous bouts. Our spirits sagged upon hearing this confession.

But no one ever doubted Ali's courage. His heart was big and his balls were even bigger. He went out for more in the sixth. Frazier, sensing the change in the tide, stepped up his attack. Joe was brutally effective. Ali sucked it up and took the punishment.

Near the end of the seventh round, Ali, with his back to the ropes, grabbed Joe by the back of the head and pulled him into a clinch. He yelled in Frazier's ear, "They told me you was washed up, champ."

Joe gritted his teeth, hammered his hardest punch to Ali's kidney, and growled, "They lied to you, champ. They lied!"

Stage two—Frazier's Turn—lasted until the end of the 10th round. By consensus, the fight was even to that point. Ali had taken the first five rounds, Frazier the second five. Ali had

Frazier in trouble early but couldn't knock him down; then Frazier had knocked Ali from one side of the ring to the other, but, he, too, had been unable to score a knockdown.

Now came the most brutal test of two equally matched human beings I have ever seen. We held on to a bit of hope in our corner. Ali is at his best when he is out on the end of a limb, we reminded ourselves. Somehow, by some unusual means, he always finds a way to win. That is why he is the definitive champion.

Frazier and his cornermen held out a similar hope. He'd beaten Ali once, so he could do it again. There were only five rounds to go. The "Championship Causeway, Route 10 to Route 15," as a fight's final rounds were sometimes called, belongs to the man who wants it the most. It is the ultimate test of wills. Ali had a strong will, but so did Joe Frazier. Who would win out in the end?

Stage three, The Shootout, began with tough trench fighting at the start of the 10th round. In the corner, before the bell, Ali had looked like a beaten man. His chin drooped on his chest. His eyes rolled back in his head when we gave him water. Bundini, his witch doctor-amateur psychologist-cheerleader, was in hysterical tears, imploring Ali, "Force yourself, champ!" Angelo calmly issued simple commands. These directives made all the boxing sense in the world to someone who wasn't fighting Joe Frazier right now and whose tank wasn't running perilously low on gas. Ali rose wearily to answer the bell for the 10th, the needle of his gas gauge hovering near E.

By Round 11, Frazier seemed at the height of his power. He fought like a devastating force of nature. He pinned Ali in a corner, where Ali stood helpless as he absorbed shot after shot.

"Lawd, have mercy!" cried Bundini on my shoulder. I could only respond, "Oh, God." Angelo continued to scream, "Get outta there. Ali, move, move." Angelo screamed again and again, but Ali stayed on the ropes, pinned there by Frazier's incessant pummeling. Joe sensed the kill.

"When Ali came to the corner, his arms went down at his sides instead of being on his lap like always," Angelo Dundee recalls. "Then I knew I had to get the ice bucket, put his head in it, and squeeze the ice on him. I knew I had to work because it was such a grueling fight. We were tired in the corner just going up and down the steps; that's how hot it was in that primitive arena with its tin roof, and the heat was multiplied with the lights. I don't know how Joe Frazier and Muhammad were able to fight that day."

In the corner Ali seemed to experience a rebirth. In sports it's called finding your second wind. In Ali's ring career it denoted the moment when the genial man-child turned into a killer. It's a frightening thing to see. When the bell rang for Round 12, the killer had emerged. He started popping his hard jab, Frazier's head bobbing back like a cork in a pool of turbulent water. Now, with Frazier bobbing and weaving and trying to deflect that jab with his gloves, Ali knew the time had come to drop his lethal right hand. Suddenly, long rights began to hammer the oncoming Frazier. Spittle and blood flew from Frazier's slack jaw. He was like a stunned, blinded bull at the end of a corrida.

As Frazier reeled to his corner, his trainer, Eddie Futch, gasped at the damage done to his man. Frazier's face had become disfigured, a mass of bumps, bruises, cuts, hickeys, and swellings. His eyes were closing.

"Can't take much more of this," said the kindly Eddie Futch to Joe.

Angelo greeted Ali with a shower of ice-cold water. Angelo was all smiles, excited by the evidence before him.

"You got him, champ. He ain't got no more power," said Dundee. Ali gave him a withering look that seemed to say, "Oh yeah? Then you go out and finish him."

Round 13 saw Ali throw every bit of his remaining strength at the sagging Frazier. Joe staggered but kept coming, barely able to see his tormentor through the slits that were his eyes. Yet still he attacked, still driving forward, throwing punches. It was an awesome display of one man's indomitable spirit. Joe Frazier would not be beaten. Ali would have to win this fight outright.

Ali continued his battering of Frazier through Round 14.

There was a palpable sense that life and death were hanging in the air in that arena. There is a limit to the amount of trauma a man's brain and body can absorb and still function. Boxers occasionally exceed this limit and, tragically, leave their lives in the ring. Tonight, amid suffocating heat and humidity, Joe Frazier had sustained a terrible beating. While his warrior heart, his implacable will, told him to go on, it remained for a saner voice to tell him that he must not.

That voice belonged to Eddie Futch, who said, "Joe, I'm going to stop it."

"No, Eddie, no. Don't do this to me," Frazier mumbled, his words barely comprehensible, uttered as they were through split lips and with a thick tongue and a clouded brain. Joe kept pleading to continue, but on this night and as always, Eddie knew best. In his quiet, authoritative voice, Futch finally said, "Sit down, son." His hand rested lightly on Joe's shoulder, preventing him from leaving the stool "It's all over," said Eddie. "The world will never forget what you did here today."

Says Angelo Dundee, "When Eddie got Joe back in the corner, he knew the guy had nothing left. He was empty. If he'd got up, he'd have got knocked out for sure. Frazier could have been hurt very easily, because in that condition, that's when a fighter gets hurt. He had nothing to go with, no resiliency."

The Thrilla in Manila was over. For two reasons it was a good thing that Eddie Futch kept Joe Frazier from coming out for another round. First, Smokin' Joe might have died in the ring. Second, Ali would have had to go out there again, too, and he might not have lasted long himself. He was near the end of his rope.

Afterward, back at the hotel when we had all recovered, Futch said, "Joe puffs up; he don't cut, but he blows up. By the 13th he could barely see. His whole face was puffed up, nicked, cut, and bruised. His face was a mess, and I wanted to stop it then, but he wanted one more round. I let him; it was his fight, he had to finish it. Also, to tell the truth, Ali hit him so much and so hard, I thought maybe he had punched himself out, so what the hell, maybe Joe had a chance. But when I seen the whipping he took and how he barely got back to the corner, I said no, it ain't worth getting his brain scrambled. He's got a fine family and a great future, and I stopped it. I ain't sorry. Joe just couldn't take one more round of that hell."

As usual, Ali summed it up best. Reclining, exhausted, on his training table in the steaming dressing room, he said, "I always bring out the best in the men I fight, but Joe Frazier, I'll tell the world right now, brings out the best in me. That's one helluva man, and God bless him."

AFTERMATH

What we saw in Manila—a fight to the finish between two great heavyweights, with intense emotion flowing; a grim battle of character and the will to win—was the fight of the century, in my book. I simply cannot think of a more entertaining fight, given all of the surrounding circumstances and the meaning of the fight to both contestants, and given its historical significance.

"What that fight goes to show you is two things," says Angelo Dundee. "Number one is that Ali was never physically the same fighter after he lost those three and a half years of his career, quite honestly. But he won two more titles because of his character, and it his character that allowed him to go on in that fight. The other thing it shows you is how bad Ali felt. He later told *Sports Illustrated* that it was the closest he ever felt to dying, and after the 10th round, when Frazier made that great comeback, he thought about quitting. So it tells you that even the great ones, they might think about quitting, but what counts is what they do."

Ali went on to be designated the athlete of the century. No one achieved his magnitude of worldwide fame. His long championship run, during which he won a heavyweight crown three times, included extraordinary fights with the toughest of opponents: Sonny

Liston, George Foreman, and Joe Frazier, among others.

Ali also was a symbol in the days of social upheaval in the sixties and seventies. He became a global hero, worshipped on every continent. He was a deeply religious man too, a man who truly loved his fellow human beings.

Ali fought on for too long. When should he have quit? Personally, I would have been ecstatic had he retired after defeating Joe Frazier in Manila. Frazier effectively retired at that point—he fought just twice more—and he is in reasonably good shape today. Frazier has continued his involvement in boxing in Philadelphia, developing young fighters including members of his family. He is revered in the sport's circles, where his stature is assured by his epic fights with Ali.

Ali suffers from mid-brain damage in the form of advanced Parkinson's disease. He handles it like he handled a tough opponent; he will not submit easily to it and in his resistance he sets a worthy example for his fellow sufferers. He travels far and wide and still captivates his audiences with his charismatic personality. He never questions God's will, and he lives enveloped by a serenity of spirit and a peace of mind that many seek but few attain.

Don King went on to become the premier promoter in boxing history. Chronically beset by legal problems and attacked by the press, he hires the best attorneys, smiles his dazzling smile, and holds his arms aloft as he cries out in his deep, sonorous voice, "Only in America!"

As for the rest of the cast from that unforgettable morning in Manila, Eddie Futch remained at the top of his profession until his death in 1999; Ali's cornermen Bundini Brown and Luis Sarria have also passed away; and Angelo Dundee remains active in boxing.

With that final fight against Frazier, Ali achieved a little-noted distinction. Through one climactic fight with each of them, Ali effectively terminated the careers of three seemingly invincible champions: Sonny Liston, George Foreman in his first incarnation, and Joe Frazier. Each fought again, more or less briefly, before calling it quits for good, but none was ever again a contender, except Foreman in his long-delayed comeback. Ali, the apparent winner of this four-way round-robin, was, ironically, the loser. He continued to fight, ultimately at the cost of his health.

For those of us who played a role in the historic sporting event that transpired in Manila on October 1, 1975, and for many of the millions who watched it on television, the fight remains unforgettable. It was the Fight of the Century.

POSTSCRIPT: ALI'S INJURY

The question that hung in the air after Manila was how much more of this type of punishment could Ali take? He had absorbed some monstrous beatings. While his opponents retired, one by one, he kept fighting. But why? Didn't we see the damage being done to him?

Did Angelo Dundee encourage him to call it quits?

"No, at no time," says Angelo, " because if I brought up the subject, he'd just say, 'I know what I'm doing.' That's Muhammad Ali. He did what he wanted to do with his life."

As his physician, I told Ali and the people around him that he should retire. I pointed out the slowing and slurring of his speech, his diminished reflexes, the beginning of a shuffling gait, and a barely perceptible thickening of his voice. These are all signs of mid-brain damage, which, when it reaches maturity, becomes the "punch-drunk syndrome." In time this syndrome usually progresses to Parkinson's disease. I voiced my concerns, but none of the members of the Ali Circus would heed my warnings, least of all Ali.

The matter of money loomed large in the background. The cost of maintaining his entourage and his growing roster of ex-wives was astronomical. Ali simply had to fight to pay off all his debts. The members of the Ali Circus were in the same straits. Not one of them had an alternative source of income commensurate with what they received when Ali fought three times a year. No one wanted to kill the Golden Goose.

It's easy to have principles and morals when you have a positive bank balance and independent wealth. It's often different when you are broke and dependent on someone else's ability to generate income.

In the mid-1970s I was a very successful doctor in Miami, with two clinics. I had made good investments and was financially secure. I would like to think that if this had not been the case and I needed Ali to keep fighting in order to support me, I would have had the moral courage to maintain my position, which was that Ali should retire.

Ignoring the subject of brain damage, the Ali Circus trundled on, with no fewer than five fights in 1976. He had fought once in 1977—winning a 15-round decision in May over the unheralded Alfredo Evangelista—when my conscience could take no more. Ali's health was deteriorating. Even the press, which is often blind to such things, noticed the worsening of his symptoms. Ali blissfully overlooked his declining boxing skills and his obvious physical impairment. But Herbert Muhammad and the rest of the boys wanted one more fight for him that year; an easy one, they emphasized.

They matched Ali up with Earnie Shavers in Madison Square Garden on September 29, 1977. Earnie Shavers! Mother of God! An easy fight? No, this fight was an act of criminal negligence. In Shavers they had picked the heaviest hitter in boxing. The man could knock down a building with one punch. Oh, he was fierce.

So much for the notion of an easy fight! The hell with it, I said to myself. This is Ali's last fight or I leave. My conscience was throbbing. They were killing this kid.

Ali waged a wonderfully courageous fight that night in the Garden. In Round 4 Shavers caught Ali with his best shot. Ali was momentarily out on his feet. He fell back against the ropes into his rope-a-dope stance. Shavers eyed him warily. Then Earnie backed off, not believing what he saw. Was Ali faking? No, he was out on his feet, in serious trouble, but once again, his habitual good luck rescued him.

The bout came down to the final round, which in those days

was the 15th. This fight was being televised by NBC, which had decided to report the judges' scoring while the fight was in progress.

Ali was ahead by three points. All he needed to do in Round 15 was box, run, and clinch, and he would win the fight. But Angelo was unaware that we were ahead by three points. He believed that the fight was very close, so he dispatched an exhausted Ali to duke it out in the last round with the heavy-fisted Shavers.

Round 15 was a battle of epic proportions, every bit as violent as Round 14 of Ali-Frazier in Manila. Both men took turns landing haymakers. The bell rang and Ali collapsed in exhaustion in the corner.

"Did I win the round?" he asked.

"Yes," someone told him.

"Did I win the fight?"

Yes, he did, by four points—much more than enough. That 15th-round war of attrition had been needless. For me this was the last straw. Slow murder, pure and simple, was being committed.

The next morning I was summoned to the New York State Athletic Commission offices, where I met a grim-faced Dr. Edwin Campbell. He held the results of lab tests in his hand.

"Ferdie, based on these results and what I saw last night, I'm recommending that we never license Ali to fight again in New York."

I smiled in relief. We both knew he was right. He showed me the lab results.

"After a tough fight like that one, you expect a little blood in the urine, but look at these tests," said Campbell. I took a look and winced.

"These results show not only whole blood cells, but entire columns of cells that line the renal tubules," he continued. "The filtration cells that strain the blood in order to produce urine are completely gone, destroyed. There is no filtration system. Ali's kidneys have been injured, and kidney damage will lead to major incapacitation and, eventually, kidney failure and death."

I made five copies of the lab report. I then sat down and wrote a formal letter. I sent copies of my letter along with the lab report to Ali; his wife, Veronica; his manager, Herbert Muhammad; his spiritual adviser and "master," the Honorable Elijah Muhammad; and, of course, Angelo Dundee.

I mailed each package separately, in a return-requested envelope, so as to be sure each person had received the message.

Everything that I experienced in boxing had occurred through the generosity and help of Angelo Dundee and, to a large extent, Chris Dundee. For years I found it hard to place any of the blame for the damage to Ali's health on Angelo. Yes, he was there. Yes, he let it happen, but in all fairness I understood why and how such a kind and loving man could not bring himself to stop Ali from committing self-destruction.

Remember, I left Ali's camp after the Shavers fight in September 1977. In December he fought an exhibition with Scott LeDoux. On February 15, 1978, Ali lost his title to a virtual amateur, Leon Spinks, in a 15-round decision in Vegas. On September 15, 1978, he won the title back from Spinks in New Orleans, by way of a 15-round decision. Both Spinks bouts were hard-fought affairs. Ali's kidneys took a beating and his brain damage progressed, yet still no one around him uttered the word *retirement*.

Ali himself, finally aware of the extent of his decline, retired in 1979. The boxing world heaved a sigh of relief. I was happy, but I knew Ali and his love of the spotlight, and I knew the parasites of the Ali Circus. In 1980, a big-money opportunity presented itself in the form of a bout in Las Vegas against one of Ali's former sparring partners, Larry Holmes, the current heavyweight champion. This fight had Major Disaster written all over it.

The over-the-hill Circus gang convened in Vegas. In my place they brought Herbert's doctor, who loaded Ali with amphetamines to lose weight; a diuretic to get the water out of his system; and, to top it all off, thyroid medication, for no discernible or justifiable reason. What little chance Ali had to win this fight evaporated amid that cocktail of pharmaceuticals, which would inexorably sap his muscular strength.

The beating inflicted by Holmes lasted into the 11th round. Ringsiders felt the fiasco should have been stopped by Round 3. I didn't think Ali should have answered the opening bell.

Let's pause for a moment to examine Angelo Dundee's reasons for sticking with Ali.

Says Angelo, "I was the manager from the get-go, and I was his trainer at the end. I'm his trainer and friend today. So I feel good about it. Our relationship was 100 percent, and it's 100 percent today. I wanted to stay there in the corner to protect him. I wasn't gonna let him get hurt. If I was there, I could stop it."

Angelo's reasoning is sound, but it doesn't jibe with the reality of what happened. If his purpose was to protect Ali, why let him fight Holmes in his drug-weakened condition? Why not stop the fight by the third round, when it was evident that Ali

Ali wooed girlfriend Veronica Porche in the Philippines and later married her. (*AP/Wide World Photos*)

had nothing to offer that night? The answer to these questions is that Angelo didn't have the power to stop the fight. That responsibility had always belonged to Herbert Muhammad and the Muslims.

They always had a lot more to lose than a fight. Ali's career was irretrievably enmeshed in his blackness and in Muslim politics. Herbert didn't have the balls to stop the Holmes fight early. Don't kid yourself: Angelo had nothing to do with it!

And if, after such a disgraceful performance, Angelo saw the light, he hid it well, for he allowed Ali to take suffer further humiliation, at the hands of a vastly inferior opponent, Trevor Berbick, who handed Ali yet another defeat, on December 11, 1981, in Nassau, the Bahamas.

And people still wonder whether Ali's brain damage is due to boxing?

Before I leave my role in the tragedy, let me try to clarify a point. Angelo Dundee is not only a close friend of mine, but the godfather of my prized daughter, Tina. We remained close after I left Ali's camp. I understood that Angelo's character is such that he could not stand up to the Muslims and leave Ali.

"If I left, Ali would have just gotten someone else and continued to fight," Angelo says, and that rationale works for him.

I say in reply, "Yes, but it's your conscience that I'm speaking of. How can you look at yourself in the mirror and say, 'I'm letting Ali go on and continue to be damaged. It's on my head. I have to live with it.'"

Such thoughts may never have passed through Angelo's head. Angelo is the baby of his family. He was programmed to obey, not to think. Older brother Chris was the boss. A tough survivor of the Depression, Chris had little sympathy for the idea of boxers quitting. They fought till they couldn't fight anymore. When Angelo picked a beautiful Georgia-born peach, Helen, a model, to be his a wife, he had two bosses he did not contradict. He also fell in love with a beautiful legend, Muhammad Ali, and he acquired another boss along the way, Herbert Muhammad and the Nation of Islam. Angelo found himself surrounded by bosses, all of them wanting or needing the Ali Circus to cruise along indefinitely.

Is there any wonder that Angelo's conscience was overwhelmed? Angelo did as he always had done: he took the path of least resistance. His rationale is weakly persuasive, but for all the wrong reasons. If Angelo was there to protect Ali from serious harm, then why was he there in Vegas for the Holmes fight, or in the Bahamas for the Berbick travesty?

Poor Angelo; he took as big a beating as Ali did, for if ever one man loved another, Angelo truly loved Ali. And no matter what kind of face he puts on it, Angelo bitterly hates what boxing did to Ali.

Thomas Hauser observes, "Ali wanted to fight. It was what he defined himself by. The three greatest fighters of all time were Muhammad Ali, Sugar Ray Robinson, and Joe Louis. All fought longer than they should have. They wound up in their later years in less than ideal condition. There's a message in that for anybody.

"But what Ali showed in Manila, more than in any other fight, was that he was a warrior. He was a gladiator. Underneath that sweet exterior was a mean, tough son of a gun at work. In that fight he said to all those people who called him a pretty boy who would fold when the going got tough, 'Here I am. This is my courage.' Ali and Joe Frazier weren't just fighting for the heavyweight championship of the world that night. They were fighting for something much more important. They were fighting for the championship of each other. They both knew that this would be the last time they would face each other, and that whoever won that night would be recognized by history as the greatest fighter."

My final observation on Ali's life is that his luck still holds for him.

He is hurting badly. His Parkinson's syndrome or disease is advancing steadily, even accelerating. Yet Ali sails blithely on, boarding one airplane after another, making appearances throughout the world, spreading hope and joy and his message that love conquers all.

How else to explain the attention and the emotions that focused on his lighting the torch at the opening ceremonies of the 1996 Olympic Games in Atlanta. This was vintage Ali. What a chance he took! What a gamble! Once more, he shocked and amazed the whole wide world. Through his electric, riveting presence, he delivered his message, "Never give up! Never! Never!"

Sugar Ray celebrated his 14th-round TKO while a disheartened Hit Man looked on. (*Hank Kaplan Archives*)

THOMAS HEARNS

VS.

SUGAR RAY LEONARD

CHAMPION   **CHAMPION**

WELTERWEIGHT CHAMPIONSHIP
(TITLE UNIFICATION BOUT)

SEPTEMBER 16, 1981
LAS VEGAS

ROUND 14

This was a fight demanded by the public. At the time of their matchup, Sugar Ray Leonard was the WBC welterweight champion, while Thomas Hearns owned the WBA welterweight crown. This fight would create a single world champion.

The two fighters had had parallel careers, each brilliant in its own way. Of the two, Sugar Ray Leonard was easily the more visible and popular. He had followed in the footsteps of Muhammad Ali, his icon. He was young, fresh, and friendly, and he could fight like a dream. Like Ali, he had made an early impression by winning an Olympic gold medal and attracting the tireless cheerleading of Howard Cosell, who saw in Sugar Ray another Ali.

Sugar Ray surrounded himself with high-quality, prime-time associates. First and foremost, he hired Angelo Dundee, who had masterminded Ali's career, to micromanage his matchmaking and supervise his training while teaching him the tricks of the professional boxing trade. Leonard enlisted one of the top boxing promoters of the seventies and eighties, Bob Arum, who had promoted several of Ali's fights. He also brought with him his own attorney, a streetwise Maryland lawyer. Team Leonard was a well-oiled, championship-bound machine.

Sugar Ray had other advantages. He possessed Ali's physical beauty, and he had an adorable young son, a miniature replica of himself, who appeared with Leonard in a series of popular TV ads. The public was squarely in Leonard's corner. For the Hearns fight Sugar Ray was naturally cast as the good guy.

Thomas "Hit Man" Hearns was another story. To begin with, his physical appearance was unusual. At 6'1" he was unusually tall for a welterweight, with broad shoulders and the wingspan of a condor. He had the longest reach of any welterweight I ever saw.

To heighten the illusion of a soaring bird of prey, Hearns boasted a tiny waist and spindly, long legs. The thin legs made him look like a flamingo. Collectively, his physical attributes created an attractive appearance. He lacked Leonard's baby-faced beauty, but his face conveyed a manly handsomeness with its prominent high cheekbones and the sloping nose of an American Indian. He had a beautiful smile, although, unlike Sugar Ray, he seldom displayed it around fight time.

Tommy Hearns was called the Hit Man and the Motor City Cobra for good reason. Most of his fights ended in knockouts. Employing his height, long reach, and punching power to devastating effect, Hearns didn't believe in wasting time. He aimed for early knockouts and usually got them. He was undefeated in 32 bouts entering the Leonard fight, having won all but two of those fights by KO.

Hearns had been groomed in a first-rate organization, Detroit's "boxing university," the Kronk Gym. The Kronk was to Detroit what the Dundees' 5th Street Gym was to Miami: a seething, crowded training ground for tough, inner-city kids. Of that pack of tough kids, Tommy Hearns was undeniably the toughest.

BACKGROUND

The fight would be held at the Caesars Palace hotel in Las Vegas and promoted by Dan Duva of Main Events Promotions. For Dan, the son of the famous boxing trainer Lou Duva, the bout was his first-ever promotion.

Dan Duva was an aggressive, boxing-oriented chip off the old block. He wanted a first-class production and the best TV coverage he could get. I was under contract to NBC, and in my view no one came close to NBC producer Mike Weisman for originality and authenticity. Dan Duva hired an almost entirely

Hearns, a product of Emanuel Steward's fabled Kronk Gym in Detroit, sparred outdoors in New York a month before his September bout with Leonard in Las Vegas. (*AP Laserphoto*)

NBC production team, with Marv Albert as the blow-by-blow announcer and me as the expert commentator. Owing to the importance of the match, and seeking a bit more pizzazz, I suggested to Weisman that we add to the team the venerable voice of televised boxing in the forties and fifties, Don Dunphy.

Dunphy was in his seventies, but still spry and sharp. The weather was predictably oppressive—100 degrees at ringside when the fight started in the afternoon. In order to spare Dunphy unnecessary exposure to the heat, we suggested that he stay in an air-conditioned trailer until the Hearns-Leonard bout was ready to start. By then the sun would have gone down, the desert would have cooled, and Dunphy would be fresh. Marv and I, in tuxedos, would sit in the 100-degree heat and call three other championship fights on the undercard. It wasn't going to be an easy day.

Our production meetings with Weisman were short, smooth, and informal. Don sat quietly, listened until we were finished, then stood up and cleared his throat. Hushed, we awaited his words; we were in awe of the master.

"I don't understand something, Mike," said Dunphy. "Marv is doing the blow-by-blow. I have been brought in to do the color analysis."

"Yes," Weisman responded.

Don turned and pointed to me. "When does he talk?"

I felt like the dancing bear. When does the bear perform? Do we really need another voice on this team?

Considering it was my idea to add Don Dunphy to the telecast, I was taken aback.

Weisman, a young man with a gentle touch, quickly and gracefully redefined our roles so that Dunphy understood his in relation to mine. To his credit, he did a great job on the telecast.

THE FIGHT

The fight, as predicted, was a blazing good one. An aggressive Tommy Hearns, seeking an early KO, stalked a retreating Sugar Ray all around the ring.

From time to time Leonard mounted a counterattack, and

meanwhile his defensive skills in retreat won him his share of rounds. But by the 10th round, however, the fight belonged to Hearns, who led by at least three points (rounds) on all of our scorecards. Dunphy pointed out that Sugar was waiting too long to make his move. In Leonard's corner Angelo Dundee was making the same point, but much more forcefully.

Viewing the tape of the fight, Mills Lane comments, "They announced that Tommy Hearns weighed in at 143½ pounds for the fight. I'm saying to myself, My God, he's a big guy. He should have weighed maybe 147 or 147½ at the first weigh-in, then gotten off the scale, walked around, spit some, taken a pee, and then got back on the scale and topped out right at 147. But when he came in more than three pounds under 147 for a 15-round fight, I thought, How's he going to do it?"

What had happened was that trainer Emanuel Steward had gradually lost control in his long relationship with Hearns. With Hearns no longer guided closely by Steward, the Hit Man's neighborhood pals infiltrated his training camp and started to call the shots. An entourage was born.

One well-meaning but amateurish friend of Hearns's took over the management of his diet, his rest, and his exercise, also encouraging the fighter to devise own training regime. This proved disastrous. The same thing had happened in Ali's last year of activity; Angelo had virtually no influence on his training habits, and the absence of a hand on the rudder showed in Ali's poor performances against Leon Spinks and thereafter.

The problem of Hearns's low weight, so aptly cited by Mills Lane, was a major factor in the fight.

"That was the key," says Emanuel Steward. "It was not any one particular punch that was a big factor in the fight as much as the situation of Tommy coming in underweight and overtrained. It was the first and only time in his entire career that that happened, and I've been involved with him since he was a little kid, 10 years old. Of course we had disputes in training, and then outside people came in and ingratiated themselves when there was a big fight coming up. There was an argument about who was running the camp, so we didn't have the harmony that we'd had before.

"During the fight, I was speaking to Thomas between the 12th and 13th rounds and all of a sudden something happened. Just like when you're on a trip and your tank suddenly runs out of gas, Thomas actually had no calories left to burn. I could see it! How he managed to fight the 13th and 14th rounds was amazing because he had nothing in his body at all."

Emanuel continues, "Normally for big fights, Thomas had always come in at about 150 pounds near the day of the fight, and he had to sweat to get his weight down to the limit. He was a big welterweight. But for that particular fight, he was a skinny welterweight. It made a difference. And he was running twice a day. He wanted to make sure he was in great shape for the fight, and we argued about his running because his weight was low. He wanted to make sure he was in the best of shape for this fight. We argued up until the day of the fight. As a result of all the work he was doing, he came in overtrained. I think that up to two days before the fight, he was still sparring. He refused to stop. When Tommy stepped on the scale (at the last weigh-in), he

Leonard, at Angelo Dundee's urging, picked up the pace of his attack after Round 12. (*Linda Platt/Hank Kaplan Archives*)

weighed 145 exactly. You could see he was skinny; he was way under-weight. Coming into the ring that night, he still weighed only about 145 pounds. He had not put on weight. As a result, we saw what happened at the end of the 12th round."

Hearns was tiring and slowing down by the start of Round 13. This was hazardous, because Leonard's fight plan, as conceived by Angelo Dundee, emphasized speed and movement. After Round 12, Angelo urged Sugar Ray to pick up the pace, and Hearns looked confused, incapable of responding to his opponent's accelerated movement. What's more, Leonard had good stamina and could punch.

"I figured that Tommy was not going to be able to just come out and bomb Ray Leonard like he did everyone else because Ray Leonard not only was a very good technical fighter, with tremendous stamina, but he always finished up strong, too," says Steward.

"I figured that Tommy would have to box very carefully, but I figured he could outbox Ray Leonard. Everyone else was looking for him to come out as a puncher. Going down the stretch, I knew Tommy had to beat the big onslaught that Ray always puts on. The fight went pretty much as I expected, except for the fact that Thomas came in too light—that was the major factor—and Ray Leonard, being the great fighter that he is, came on strong and everything went right for him at the right time."

Angelo Dundee offers the view from Leonard's corner after 12 rounds had been contested: "I saw my guy was slowing up, like Hearns was slowing up," says Angelo. "I figured the way Ray wins is with his speed, by picking up the pace. Move, move, move. Pop a right, slide over. So I slap his legs and do a little yelling, you know: 'This is for the championship, baby.' And Ray responds. He gets on his bicycle and he goes."

As Round 13 got under way, Hearns was looking tired and perplexed. His legs no longer glided smoothly across the canvas. Leonard was the opposite, circling the ring as if on roller skates. Suddenly, Sugar Ray hit Hearns with a hard right to the ribs, and the Hit Man seemed to collapse as he slid along the ropes. Don Dunphy and I looked at each other quizzically. The punch hadn't seemed so hard; indeed, it had appeared to glance off Hearns's side. Nevertheless, Hearns was in obvious trouble, and Leonard sprang to the attack.

Sugar Ray threw a stiff shot that caught Hearns on the top of his head. Hearns seemed seriously staggered by the blow, but once again, Dunphy and I were dubious. To us, the punch appeared not to have caught its target flush. What was happening?

Now Leonard warmed to the assault, driving Hearns through the ropes. Referee Davey Pearl had reached eight in his count when Hearns clambered back into the ring. The bell then sounded, saving the injured Hit Man, who looked like a whipped fighter as he lurched to his corner on weakened legs. Steward doused him with cold water and then began desperately to revive his fighter for the next round.

"That was it right there. Tommy was out of gas," says Emanuel. "It wasn't that the body blow was so powerful, as the fact that Tommy had no stamina to resist it. He caved in and slid along the ropes. I thought about stopping it, but we were ahead (on points) with only two rounds to go."

The 14th round beckoned. Sugar Ray smelled the title. Hearns's corner was a mass of confusion; someone failed to bring in the ring stool until the between-rounds break was almost over.

"Tommy was out of it, but only six minutes remained," Emanuel Steward observes. "Even if we lost both rounds 10 points to 9, we would have won the fight. It was a tough choice. I would not have objected to stopping it, but Tommy, game as ever, wanted to go on."

On the opposite side of the ring, Angelo Dundee and his fighter sensed that the end was near for Thomas Hearns. "Tommy was ready to go (down), and Ray knew it," says Angelo. "I didn't have to yell or slap Ray's legs this time. No one ever had to tell Ray when to close the show."

Sensing victory, Sugar Ray, his face and eyes puffy, began to chase a retreating Hearns in earnest. It seemed to us that Leonard had turned on all his switches, while Tommy's switches were being dimmed one by one at the same time. But Hearns was still comfortably ahead on everyone's scorecard. He could afford to lose a round while he recuperated from that rib shot.

Sometimes a boxer's corner makes a difference in a close fight. That was never more evident than in this bout. When Hearns went down and, at the bell, staggered to his corner, badly in need of resuscitation, he was met by confusion and disarray. Someone had forgotten to bring his stool into the corner. Emanuel Steward was forced to waste precious seconds getting his cornermen to perform their work. Meanwhile, Hearns stood unattended. In the opposite corner, Angelo Dundee's streamlined machine clicked smoothly, preparing Sugar Ray for the kill that Angelo felt was imminent.

Hearns was holding his own, losing this 14th round but punching back when attacked. The crucial difference was that Sugar Ray appeared to be getting stronger and Hearns weaker. There was definitely a hunter and a quarry in the ring, and for Hearns, the prey, time was running out, along with his sagging spirit.

At 1:48 in the round Sugar Ray landed a wild, looping right, which appeared only to graze Hearns's jaw, but the Hit Man slumped on the ropes, sliding along the strands as he attempted to regain his balance. Sugar Ray closed quickly on him, raking him with 14 unanswered punches before Hearns responded feebly with a weak combination.

Now Sugar had cornered Hearns. He landed three solid shots, one of them a devastating hook to Hearns's ribs. Tommy's long legs seemed to buckle, but he remained upright, his gloves held high, next to his head. He was in big trouble. Then, all of a sudden, out of nowhere, referee Davey Pearl stopped the fight! Sugar Ray Leonard had stopped Tommy Hearns and was now the undisputed welterweight champion!

Don Dunphy and I were disbelieving. Why? we wondered. Hearns wasn't counted out, he wasn't down, he had his gloves up, and he did manage to punch back. What's more, Hearns presumably was leading on the scorecards. Why had this fight, a title bout of such importance, been stopped by the ref?

Here is Emanuel Steward's take on what happened.

"Was the call right? You didn't see me complaining," says Emanuel. "Never in all the years since that fight have I questioned Davey Pearl's call. That is primarily because I knew of Tommy's exhausted condition. I doubt if Tommy could have answered the bell for the 15th round. I was ready to throw in the towel. So was Pearl's decision correct? Absolutely. Yes."

Unaware of what Hearns's corner knew so well—that their fighter was overtrained, perilously underweight, and, now, exhausted—Dunphy and I were livid. With a century of boxing experience between us, we could point to many come-back-from-oblivion-to-win title bouts. People like Jake LaMotta received terrific beatings, only to come back and win through sheer grit. We knew that Tommy Hearns was a courageous fighter, and he had one-punch knockout power. What if Sugar Ray had punched himself out? What if Tommy could summon up some of that reserve gas tank that Ali somehow would always find—that second wind to ride through a last-gasp offensive? What then? We will never know, and in the light of Emanuel Steward's "untold story," we now know that Davey Pearl was right. It was all over!

Mills Lane offers a referee's perspective on the matter. "Pearl's decision was a judgment call, a close thing," Mills says. "It was a very big, important fight. Hearns was ahead, but there was a bit more than one minute to go to the end of the (14th) round. Hearns had his gloves up, but he was taking a beating from Sugar Ray, who was stepping up the pressure.

"Now, was it worth risking Tommy's health, if not his life? Could Tommy have made it to the bell? Was he so exhausted and hurt that he had no chance of surviving one more three-minute round?

"Pearl's choice was made in a split second, in the heat of the action. The main consideration was Tommy taking too much punishment. Did he have anything left? Davey Pearl, in my opinion, made the right choice.

"Would I have done the same? Probably not. I would have given Tommy a while longer, but that is nit-picking. Tommy had lost the fight, period. In my book, Davey Pearl did a fine job and stopped the fight when he saw fit."

AFTERMATH

Sugar Ray reached the top of his profession, but then a series of quirky events sidetracked his career. First, he suffered a detached retina. The injury was repaired , but its effects caused him to retire twice in five years, during which time he fought only once, against Kevin Howard, whom he defeated on a ninth-round TKO in May 1984. When he did come back, it was in the role of underdog in a fight with the reigning middleweight champion, Marvelous Marvin Hagler. The fight was a corking good scrap. Once again, the corners influenced the fight's outcome. In Leonard's corner the reliable Angelo Dundee was screaming and cursing, doing whatever was needed to keep Leonard's engine revving high. In Hagler's corner his managers, the brothers Goody and Pat Petronelli, had long ago relinquished control to the fighter himself. Hagler didn't like to hear negative comments about his performance. By assuring him that everything was fine and going in his favor, his handlers caused Hagler to give away important rounds to the stoked-up Leonard.

Especially disastrous for Hagler was Round 15. The Petronellis spent time in the corner following the 14th telling him to box cautiously. They were sure they were ahead on points, and Hagler would be foolish to fight aggressively and risk being knocked out.

Across the ring, Angelo Dundee employed a time-honored strategy. "We're behind, son," he advised Leonard. "We need this round to win."

Angelo was right. The Petronellis were wrong.

Sugar Ray won the 15th round and stole a split decision.

Tommy Hearns had a long and honorable career, winning multiple titles in more than one weight division. He finally got a rematch with Sugar Ray on June 12, 1989, but by then both men were fighting only from memory. Hearns dropped Leonard twice, but somehow the judges ruled it a draw.

Even as late as 1999, Hearns continued to fight, while Sugar Ray stirred fitfully on the sidelines, considering one last comeback.

This is so typical of great fighters that I am reminded of a conversation I had with Leonard after one of his first professional fights. He had followed Ali's career closely, so he knew me as Muhammad's fight doctor and the man who had pleaded with Ali to quit before it was too late.

"Doc, you'll never have to tell me to quit," said Sugar Ray. "The first clear million I have in the bank, I'll be gone."

"We'll see," I said, shaking my head. Oh, if it were only so. But it wasn't. It never is.

Hearns and Hagler sported their ornamental championship belts before the big bout. (*Hank Kaplan Archives*)

MARVELOUS MARVIN HAGLER
MIDDLEWEIGHT CHAMPION

VS.

THOMAS HEARNS
WELTERWEIGHT CHAMPION

APRIL 15, 1985
LAS VEGAS

ROUND 1

The mid-eighties saw the nation percolating along, with prosperity on the rise. The sports scene, buoyed by rapidly developing cable television systems, became a major economic force in the United States.

By mid-1985, with pay-per-view an economic juggernaut, the boxing public clamored for a dream fight. The middleweight division, second only to the heavyweight class, is traditionally a favorite with the fans. At this time two middleweights had blossomed into superstardom, and a meeting between them was eagerly anticipated.

In Marvelous Marvin Hagler boxing fans had a rough, tough spoiler from Brockton, Massachusetts. Hagler's main problem was that no one in his right mind wanted to fight a left-handed, heavy-punching, iron-jawed, determined brawler like himself. Marvelous Marvin Hagler had fought and beaten the best. His fights were always exciting, as he battled with the self-assurance of a man who felt he couldn't be beaten and who knew he had the knockout power to end matters quickly. Moreover,

Hagler was a "protected" fighter when he performed in New England. An opponent was unlikely to win a decision in or around Boston, where the Petronelli brothers, who were Hagler's managers, and Sol Silberman, his promoter, were entrenched. If your fighter was going up against Marvelous Marvin in New England, you were advised to heed the admonition of Hagler's cornerman Freddie Brown: "When you're out of town, you're out of town."

Tommy Hearns was also a knockout puncher, but the Leonard fight had left a lingering question mark concerning the strength of his chin. Hearns entered the fight as an underdog. Although he was a formidable welterweight, he was moving up in weight to confront the very best fighter around.

"The night of the fight, right before the opening bell, I picked Hagler to win by a KO inside three rounds," says Angelo Dundee. "I just felt that Hearns couldn't take a big middleweight punch. I always felt that a great middleweight could beat a great welterweight."

The protagonists performed some promotional work for the closed-circuit telecast. (*AP Laserphoto/Ed Bailey*)

While I basically agree with Angelo, I am bemused by his view, since his own great welterweight, Carmen Basilio, beat the great middleweight Sugar Ray Robinson, capturing Robinson's middleweight title in 1957. (Robinson won a rematch the following year.) In the sixties and seventies Angelo steered the great Cuban welterweight Luis Manuel Rodriguez to victories over such middleweight stars as Hurricane Carter (twice), Wilbert "Skeeter" McClure, and Denny Moyer, and even a light-heavyweight, Vicente Rondon, who went on to become a world champion. Of course, when the role of great middleweight is filled by Marvelous Marvin Hagler, I can understand clearly what Angelo Dundee is talking about. Not surprisingly, Hagler went into the fight solidly favored by the fight crowd and the bookies.

Janks Morton, who trained Sugar Ray Robinson and was a close observer of Hearns, says, "Tommy couldn't handle gaining the weight and still maintain mobility. Standing still, Hagler would KO him. Tommy didn't have the strength for Hagler."

But Emanuel Steward, Hearns's tutor, confidant, manager and trainer, saw the solution that might enable the Hit Man to prevail. "Tommy had a perfect punch to counter a left-hander who comes straight in: a right-hand counter to nail him as he's coming in. Tommy would depend on his powerful right to stop Hagler coming in," says Steward.

Says veteran trainer Lou Duva: "Hagler had strength, not speed. Tommy was much faster, and a better boxer. Hagler's fight was all pressure, pressure, pressure—make Tommy fight going backward."

THE FIRST ROUND

The opening round began with a blistering exchange. Both fighters came out firing punches; there was no tactical dancing tonight. Both men staked out a position in the middle of the ring and commenced winging their best shots. Many of the hard punches landed, and the audience gasped in surprise at the ferocity of the action barely after the round had started. Nobody was supposed to be able to take clean left hooks by Hagler, but here was Hearns doing just that. No fighter alive should be able to absorb Hearns's walloping right-hand counters, but that's what Hagler was doing.

The first man to waver was, surprisingly, Hagler. By the 30-second mark he was in trouble—not desperate trouble, just "wobble" trouble. Hearns, a killer finisher, went to a two-handed attack in hopes of scoring a quick KO, but that result eluded him. Soon the snap seemed to evaporate from his powerful right-hand punches. They continued to land, but they were now slaps more than shots.

Both fighters threw and received some low blows, but amid the breakneck pace the referee didn't bother to issue even a warning. Indeed, the action was unfolding so furiously fast that the ref had no chance to intervene, so he did what a good referee is supposed to do: he stayed out of the way, leaving the fighters to resolve their battle alone and uninterrupted.

Hagler had fully recovered by the middle of the round, which saw each man pounding body shots upon the other. Hagler began landing his devastating left hook almost at will, while Hearns depended on big, straight right-hand counters. After two minutes, however, Hearns suddenly seemed tired. Exhaustion, frustration, bewilderment were etched on his face. Could he fend off Hagler's savage attack and survive the duration of the round? As fans pondered this question, a piece of good luck fell right into the Hit Man's pocket: Marvelous Marvin had a cut on the bridge of his nose.

The round's final minute seemed to last an eternity. From somewhere within himself, Tommy Hearns found a hidden storehouse of guts, resiliency, and a gambler's willingness to go for broke. Meanwhile, the cut on his nose had covered Hagler's face with blood.

Bloodied but hardly bowed, Marvin Hagler felt he was in command, felt the tide of battle turning in his favor. Far from looking worn-out or weary, Hagler looked fresh, as if he were enjoying every minute of his bit of exercise. It was now his turn to attack, and he raced in to finish the grueling round with a flurry. Hearns fought back, matching Marvin blow for blow, when suddenly, with just nine seconds left, a smashing combination by Hagler buckled him. Hearns fell into the ropes and Hagler charged forward, sensing a knockout, but the bell saved Tommy Hearns.

At that instant everyone present in Caesars Palace breathed a sigh of relief and then burst into spontaneous applause. A standing ovation swept through the arena. It was a remarkable show of appreciation for what I, along with millions of others, consider the greatest single round of boxing in the history of the fight game.

Hearns was living on borrowed time after that furious first round. Round 2 was a hard-fought battle—won by Hagler—and the third round was the fight's last. Hagler unleashed three vicious rights, sending the Hit Man crashing to the canvas. The ref had seen enough, and signaled a knockout. Marvelous Marvin was the winner and still the champion.

BOXING EXPERTS SPEAK

Here is how George Benton, the crafty onetime middleweight contender who became a boxing trainer and manager, saw the round: "Hagler felt Tommy had a weak chin and could be knocked out, so he decided to stick close to Hearns and roll the dice. If you got a man that can punch like Hearns, then you got to stick close and shoot the dice. Hagler got as close to Tommy Hearns as a man gets to his underwear."

The great Archie Moore, who once fought nearly as memorable a round with Yvon Durelle, sat in admiration as he watched this one on tape. "That's the most active round of fighting I've ever seen," he said. "Both men could have been knocked out by any one punch. Both showed a champion's heart. Neither man would quit."

Angelo Dundee adds, "That is without question the best I ever saw Tommy Hearns fight. It simply don't get better than that first round. What held up Hagler, I don't know. How Tommy didn't fold, I don't know. I do know it's the best round I ever saw."

THE UNTOLD STORY

Emanuel Steward recently reexamined this historic round—his own well-conceived plan of attack, the unexpected complications that instantly changed the fight's momentum, and what exactly had happened to Tommy Hearns. Emanuel had remained silent on this latter "secret" at the request of Hearns, who didn't want to appear to be making an excuse and thereby taking credit away from Marvelous Marvin Hagler.

"I've known Marvin Hagler since 1973, when he was an amateur, and Marvin was always a good, solid fighter," says Emanuel. "He had a lot of emotions pent up inside him because he felt that he had never gotten the right break. Earlier in his career, he had to fight a lot of Philadelphia fighters in Philadelphia, and they had a tournament going on once and they wouldn't let him in. Anyway, he became a very complete fighter, and I knew this was going to be a very hard fight for Hearns.

"But Tommy trained very hard for the fight and was in excellent condition. Not to find any excuse for him, but Marvin devised a great plan. I think it was the only plan that would be effective. Later on, when Marvin and I spoke about it, he said, 'Emanuel, I knew I could not box Tommy Hearns. I saw how good he could box. I also knew Tommy punched harder than I did, and the only way I could fight was to try and make it an all-out brawl—fight at close quarters, keep my chin as close as I could to my chest, and be very physical, because in all other areas Tommy was superior to me.' And Marvin fought a great fight.

"Prior to the fight, some friends of his had massaged Tommy's legs. While I was downstairs at the gym, dealing with a problem, all the guys from his neighborhood in Detroit were at his feet, and when I came back, I found they had massaged his legs. I ran them out of the room, and Tommy didn't understand why I was so upset. I know what a massage does to legs prior to an event. Nevertheless, as we're getting ready to go to the fight, Tommy says, 'I don't know why my legs feel so weak, why I'm so tired.' I didn't say anything because I knew Hagler was going to come at him with the fury that he always unleashed as soon as the bell rang. Tommy didn't need anything else to worry about."

Steward continues, "So Tommy goes into the fight with his legs already hurt. Marvin comes out and jumps on Tommy right away. Tommy being Tommy, he stood and hit him with a right hand that Marvin told us later on was the hardest he was ever hit in his career. Marvin acted like he was hurt, staggering and holding on. And then, after

Marvelous Marvin's headgear foretold what would transpire in the first round. (*AP Laserphoto/Reed Saxon*)

that, Tommy came to the corner at the end of the first round and said, 'I broke my hand.' I said, 'What?' Tommy said, 'I broke my right hand. It's broke.'

"The rest of that fight, I'm looking at a disaster between the leg problem and the hand and the way that Marvin was coming to him. Tommy actually couldn't box if he wanted to, because Marvin was crowding him, plus his legs were already weakened from the massage. So he just stood toe to toe, and if you look at the tape you'll see he was landing right hands, but they were almost like clubbing right hands. They were not really the straight power punches that he usually shoots straight down the middle and turns his weight into, because he couldn't do that"

I asked, "Why wasn't Tommy using his left hand to jab, hook, go to the body? His right hand was now virtually useless; it had no effectiveness."

Emanuel replied, "Well, first of all, Tommy don't fight this close and Marvin is making him fight very close, which is very smart. Then there is the fact that Tommy's legs are hurting. He can't move that much. So he himself has to fight at fairly close range.

"You know, when we got back in the dressing room after the fight, Tommy said, 'Did the fans enjoy the fight? 'Cause I saw it was a good fight. Can you apologize for all of us for losing? And when we go out into the press conference, don't mention anything about my right hand being broke because Marvin fought a great fight. He laid out a good plan, it worked, the fans got their money's worth, and we don't do anything to take away from his glory.' That was typical Tommy."

Mills Lane concurs that this round was historic. "That was the best single round that I have ever seen, maybe the best round of the century," he says. "I have never seen a round as competitive as that round's give-and-take, with both of them banging, both of them with their plans. But you know, Marvin Hagler's people have asked me who was the most complete fighter I ever saw. When you talk about dedication, discipline, attending to business, training, doing what had to be done, Hagler was as complete a machine as I have ever seen."

Steward takes no issue with Lane's assessment. "Marvin was a great fighter," says Steward. "He could have adjusted to whatever style was necessary. If he fought someone that was shorter, he became a consummate boxer. If he fought a tall guy like Tommy, he would become a slugger. He could do anything in the book."

Finally, Lou Duva, who in more than half a century's involvement in boxing has managed 16 boxers to world titles, adds this evaluation of Marvelous Marvin Hagler:

"He was a tough southpaw who brought lots of pressure. You had to fight with him or run out of the ring. He hit you all over your body, all over your head. He was strong and he was one good fighter. Could he take a punch? Sure he could take a punch. If you opened up his head you would find one thing: a big boxing glove."

AFTERMATH

Tommy Hearns continued to fight on, but this bout finished him as a great boxer. He left it all in that ring that night, or rather, Hagler took it all from him. Sadly, despite all of Emanuel Steward's efforts to prevent it, Tommy has fought on, ignoring the truth and risking further damage to his injured brain. Hearns thus joined the legion of great champions—Sugar Ray Robinson, Roberto Duran, and others—who by foolishly continuing to fight not only defraud the public, but, more important, damage themselves. In persisting they are dooming themselves to a life of dimmed vision, thickened voice, shuffling feet, and the ultimate sequel of mid-brain damage, Parkinson's disease.

More happily, Marvelous Marvin Hagler discovered a new career in Italy, that of a movie actor, and has made several entertaining films. In retirement Marvin is a peaceful, satisfied warrior. He entertains no aspirations to return to the ring; no rematches with Hearns or Leonard. He laughs at the idea when it's brought up. In my view he ranks right up there with Sugar Ray Robinson and Carlos Monzon among the best middleweights of the 20th century.

Unanimity in the boxing fraternity that the opening round of the Marvelous Marvin Hagler vs. Thomas "Hit Man" Hearns title bout remains the greatest round of the 20th century reinforces what I believe: Marvin Hagler is not only up there with the likes of Robinson and Monzon. He is the best.

AFTERWORD: HOW I RANK THE ROUNDS

For centuries boxing has intrigued and thrilled fans with its unique blend of man-to-man competition, guile, brutality, technique, strategy, and suspense. Having described my choices of the 12 greatest rounds ever fought, I now offer, in conclusion, my rankings of those dozen historic rounds, from bottom to top.

12. **The St. Valentine's Day Massacre**, Round 13, Sugar Ray Robinson vs. Jake LaMotta, February 14, 1951. Boxing's best pound-for-pound fighter triumphs in a bloody battle.

11. **A Matter of Timing**, Round 13, Rocky Marciano vs. Jersey Joe Walcott, September 23, 1952. Marciano, who would retire undefeated, wins the heavyweight crown he would never relinquish.

10. **The Phantom Punch**, Round 1, Muhammad Ali vs. Sonny Liston, May 25, 1965. In a brief, bizarre rematch, Liston, convinced that Ali is crazy, gets knocked down and decides to stay down.

9. **The Comeback Kid**, Round 14, Thomas Hearns vs. Sugar Ray Leonard, September 16, 1981. Leonard becomes the undisputed welterweight champ when referee Davey Pearl suddenly stops the fight.

8. **Conn's Gamble**, Round 13, Joe Louis vs. Billy Conn, June 18, 1941. Ahead on points, Conn makes an ill-fated decision to slug it out with the Brown Bomber.

7. **The Long Count**, Round 7, Jack Dempsey vs. Gene Tunney, September 22, 1927. In one of boxing's most memorable bouts, a controversial count enables Tunney to survive a knockdown and go on to win a 10-round decision.

6. **The Blind Round**, Round 5, Cassius Clay vs. Sonny Liston, February 24, 1964. The future Muhammad Ali demonstrates his perseverance and captures the heavyweight title in a huge upset.

5. **The Massacre**, Round 1, Jack Dempsey vs. Jess Willard, July 4, 1919. The Manassa Mauler inflicts a shockingly savage beating en route to winning the heavyweight crown.

4. **The Rumble in the Jungle**, Round 8, Muhammad Ali vs. George Foreman, October 30, 1974. Ali, back from exile, unveils the rope-a-dope and KOs the previously unbeaten Foreman.

3. **The Revenge**, Round 1, Joe Louis vs. Max Schmeling, June 22, 1938. The great Joe Louis decisively wins a rematch with the whole world watching.

2. **The Thrilla in Manila**, Round 14, Muhammad Ali vs. Joe Frazier, October 1, 1975. In a life-and-death struggle that was, for my money, the fight of the century, Ali is the last man standing.

1. **War**, the greatest round of the century, Round 15, Marvelous Marvin Hagler vs. Thomas Hearns, April 15, 1985. Hagler, as good a fighter as ever stepped into a ring, prevails after a furious opening round in which two men threw everything they had at each other.

These are my picks. Others might rank these rounds differently—or choose entirely different rounds as the greatest ever—but I think we can agree that these 12 rounds deserve a place in the annals of boxing and will not be forgotten by those who witnessed them.

INDEX

ABOUT THE AUTHORS

Ferdie Pacheco, M.D., "the Fight Doctor," is a physician, boxing analyst, author, screenwriter, and fine artist. After serving for 15 years as Muhammad Ali's physician and cornerman, in 1977 he began a career as a boxing analyst for major television networks; he currently works on major productions of Showtime Championship Boxing. He received an Emmy Award for 1989–90 for his work on a series of specials on Ali's greatest fights. He has written or contributed to several books, including *Muhammad Ali: A View from the Corner*. He lives in Miami with his wife, the flamenco artist Luisita Sevilla.

Jim Moskovitz is the cowriter and executive producer of the companion Showtime television special "The 12 Greatest Rounds of Boxing: The Untold Stories." He is the creator, cowriter, and executive producer of television's weekly *Tim McCarver Show* and the creator and producer of Tim McCarver's national radio program, *Talking Sports*. He created, wrote, and produced long-running radio series with Pat Summerall and Ron MacLean and was a cowriter of the book *Pat Summerall's Sports in America*. He created, directed, cowrote, and was executive producer of a television special, "Grand Slam," that received two Sports Video of the Year Awards. He also developed the motion picture *The Boys of Summer*.

Mills Lane is a prominent and widely respected boxing referee, a former district court judge in Nevada, and the host of the televised courtroom show *Judge Mills Lane*.